ISBN 978-1-331-41736-1
PIBN 10187284

1 MONTH OF
FREE
READING

at

www.ForgottenBooks.com

By purchasing this book you are eligible for one month membership to ForgottenBooks.com, giving you unlimited access to our entire collection of over 700,000 titles via our web site and mobile apps.

To claim your free month visit:

www.forgottenbooks.com/free187284

English
Français
Deutsche
Italiano
Español
Português

www.forgottenbooks.com

Mythology Photography **Fiction**
Fishing Christianity **Art** Cooking
Essays Buddhism Freemasonry
Medicine **Biology** Music **Ancient**
Egypt Evolution Carpentry Physics
Dance Geology **Mathematics** Fitness
Shakespeare **Folklore** Yoga Marketing
Confidence Immortality Biographies
Poetry **Psychology** Witchcraft
Electronics Chemistry History **Law**
Accounting **Philosophy** Anthropology
Alchemy Drama Quantum Mechanics
Atheism Sexual Health **Ancient History**
Entrepreneurship Languages Sport
Paleontology Needlework Islam
Metaphysics Investment Archaeology
Parenting Statistics Criminology
Motivational

THE CASE

AGAINST

PROFESSOR BRIGGS

PART II.

NEW YORK

CHARLES SCRIBNER'S SONS

1893

THE CASE

AGAINST

PROFESSOR BRIGGS

DR. BRIGGS' WORKS

THE CASE

AGAINST

PROFESSOR BRIGGS

PART II.

NEW YORK

CHARLES SCRIBNER'S SONS

1893

TABLE OF CONTENTS.

THE PRELIMINARY OBJECTION OF PROF. BRIGGS TO
THE STATUS OF THE COMMITTEE OF PROSECUTION,
NOVEMBER 9TH, 1892; THE ACTION OF THE PRESBY-
TERY OF NEW YORK THEREON; AND THE COMPLAINT
OF PROF. BRIGGS TO THE SYNOD OF NEW YORK.

A. *The preliminary objection of Prof. Briggs, Nov. 9,
1892, to the status of the Committee of Prosecution.*

Dr. BRIGGS—I rise at this stage to make a preliminary objection which it is necessary for me to make
here in order to maintain my rights of objecting to this
committee in the status that it claims at the present
time. I cannot permit them to act as a prosecuting
committee until I challenge their right so to act, and
have the Presbytery pass upon my preliminary objections.

I do not mean to take up much time at present—no
more than is absolutely necessary to bring the case in a
proper form before the house. I was in hopes that the
Synod of New York would decide their status at its last
meeting by entertaining the complaint filed by 114 ministers and elders of the Presbytery; but the Synod did
not take action upon the complaint, and virtually re-
turned the matter to the Presbytery for reconsideration.
The responsibility is thrown upon me, therefore, as an
original party to again bring this question before the
Presbytery. I cannot shirk it.

It is far from my intention to put any obstruction in the way of a course of procedure prescribed by the General Assembly. So far as I am concerned, it need take but a very short time to determine this preliminary objection. I would indeed prefer to do no more at this stage than to state that I have several objections to the status of the Committee and to ask the privilege of presenting them immediately after the Presbytery has passed upon the sufficiency of the charges and specifications again to be submitted by order of the General Assembly; but it is necessary in order that I may do this that the Moderator should decide that I may then have that right and that the prosecution should consent to this order; otherwise I am obliged to file these objections at once. I wait for a decision on this question.

The MODERATOR—The Moderator's decision is, that this question had better be decided now rather than later.

Dr. BRIGGS—In order to save the time of the house and in order to save, so far as possible, any argument on this question, I have prepared a very brief statement of the history of the procedure leading up to our present situation, which I will read and then I will read the objections. I hope it will not take more than seven or eight minutes.

Let me briefly review the history of the case leading up to the present situation. The Committee appointed by the Presbytery May 12, 1891, " to arrange and prepare the necessary proceedings appropriate in the case of Dr. Briggs," presented charges and specifications against me at the meeting of Presbytery, October 5, 1891. These were served upon me on that date, and I was cited to appear and plead to these charges and specifications on November 4, 1891. On that day I filed objections to the sufficiency of the charges in form and legal effect.

The Presbytery, after hearing these objections, dismissed the case against me. A motion was then made to discharge the Committee. This motion was ruled out of order by the Moderator on the ground that the Presbytery had previously decided that this Committee was a Prosecuting Committee, an original party, and virtually and practically independent of the Presbytery. The Presbytery had made this decision on appeal from the decision of this question by the Moderator, and had sustained the Moderator by a vote of 64 to 57. Notice of complaint was given by Dr. Brown and others, which complaint was subsequently, and before it was presented to the Synod, signed by 114 ministers and elders of the Presbytery, 67 of whom had voted on the motion to sustain the Moderator; showing that the Moderator had been sustained by a mistake and misapprehension on the part of at least ten voters. This complaint, according to the law of complaints, ought to have acted as a stay to all further proceeding until the Synod had determined the complaint. The Committee, whose status was thus questioned, gave notice of appeal to Synod, but subsequently changed their appeal to the General Assembly. This appeal was prosecuted before the last General Assembly at Portland, Oregon, the Committee disregarding the law of the stay of complaints, and preferring to bring their *ex parte* statement before the General Assembly, when by the law of the Church the complainants could only appear before the Synod.

The law of the Church makes the defendant the appellee in the case. I was therefore obliged to appear before the General Assembly and resist the entertainment of the appeal, and then, after the appeal had been entertained, to oppose the sustaining of the appeal. This was a difficult task for the appellee, for the reason that the Presbytery did not do what he requested them to do in the objections which he filed, which was simply and alone to declare the charges and specifications insufficient in form and legal effect, but the Presbytery buried the original motion to dismiss the case on the ground of his paper under a number of irrelevant amendments which were not in his interest and which weakened in no inconsiderable degree the value of the dismissal in the estimation of the defendant; nevertheless compelled by law to defend this action, I did it to the best of my ability.

I was also embarrassed in my defense of the action of the Presbytery by the fact that the Presbytery had officially recognized the Committee as a Committee of Prosecution by sustaining the Moderator in his decision of that status, and that the complaint, signed by a majority of the Presbytery, was to come before the Synod, requesting the Synod to reverse the mistaken action of the Presbytery. In view of all these circumstances, I refrained from raising the question of the status of the Committee before the General Assembly, and I, again and again, expressly reserved that question for consideration by the Synod. This question, therefore, did not come before the Assembly for action. The General Assembly, therefore, took no action relating to the status of the Committee, but, after recognizing their appeal to be in order, first decided to entertain the appeal, and then to sustain the appeal in all its specifications of error. The General Assembly then reversed the action of the Presbytery in dismissing the case. This is their judgment: "The case is remanded to the Presbytery of New York for a new trial, with directions to proceed to pass upon and determine the sufficiency of the charges and specifications," as has been read to you a moment ago.

At the meeting of the Presbytery in October last this day was appointed for the new trial. In the meanwhile the Synod had taken no action on the complaint. They found the complaint to be in proper form, but resolved that it was inexpedient to take action at the present time, for the following reasons: " First, the case, through the action of the General Assembly and the Presbytery of New York, is again before the Presbytery, and the complainants may there have their remedy in their own hands. Second, in case the remedy there be found insufficient, they will afterwards have opportunity by appeal or complaint to bring the case again before the Synod."

It is evident, therefore, that by the direction of the General Assembly the Presbytery enters upon a new trial with two specific directions: to do what the appellants charged the Presbytery with not doing at the previous trial, first, to decide on the question of sufficiency, and second, to permit amendment if the interests of justice require it.

The Committee also appear before you in a status differing materially from their status when they preferred the charges in October, 1891. They now claim to be a Committee of Prosecution, to be an original party, and to be independent of this Presbytery; and yet they are confronted with the advice of the Synod to the complainants that they should again test the status of the Committee in this Presbytery, in order that, if the complainants still remain in the majority, the Committee may be discharged, as was originally proposed, or if they should be in the minority, they may bring their matters by appeal or complaint before the Synod at the next meeting.

These, then, are my objections. I do hereby submit

to the Presbytery the following objections to the procedure:

First. A Committee originally appointed "to arrange and prepare the necessary proceedings appropriate in the case of Dr. Briggs" appears before you claiming to be a Committee of Prosecution, and they are recognized as such by the Moderator's giving them the floor to act in that capacity. But their right so to act is legally questioned by complaint to the Synod of New York, and it has not yet been lawfully determined by the Synod.

Second. This Committee appeared before the last General Assembly as an original party, and acted as such by presenting an appeal against the judgment of the Presbytery in dismissing the case against me. They now appear before you as an original party successful in their appeal. Their right to act as an original party is questioned in the said complaint, and it has not yet been lawfully determined by the Synod.

Third. This Committee claim to represent the Presbyterian Church in the United States of America, and to be independent of this Presbytery which appointed them. They acted independently of the Presbytery by appealing to the General Assembly against the judgment of the Presbytery in dismissing the case against me. They now appear before you with a reversal of the judgment of the Presbytery which they have obtained. Their right to act independently of the Presbytery is questioned in the said complaint, and it has not yet been lawfully determined by the Synod.

Fourth. This Committee appear before you having acted, as is claimed, in violation of the constitution of the Church, which provides that when a complaint has been signed by more than one-third of those present and voting in the Presbytery, it acts as a stay to further proceedings. The above-mentioned complaint, signed by a majority of the voters, has been filed with the Synod of New York, and has been found in order by the Synod of New York, and is now in possession of the Synod of New York. Until the questions raised in said complaint have been determined, this Committee cannot legally take any action in the matters complained of. They cannot act as a Prosecuting Committee, or as an original party, or as independent of the Presbytery; and you cannot allow them so to act without a violation of the law of complaint embedded in the constitution of the Church.

Inasmuch as the Synod of New York suggested that the complainants, being according to the number of signers in the complaint, a majority of the Presbytery, may have the remedy in their own hands, the Presbytery are respectfully requested to apply the said remedy and, in accordance with the provision of the Book of Discipline, to determine these preliminary objections which I hereby file.   C. A. BRIGGS.

B. *The action of the Presbytery on this objection.*

Dr. BRIGGS—I do not wish to argue this case, and I hope the prosecution will allow it to go before the Presbytery to be determined without argument. Of course, if the other side insist upon argument I reserve my right of reply.

[At this point Elder John J. McCook rose and argued elaborately against Dr. Briggs, pp. 27–44 of Stenographer's Report.]

Dr. ROBERT R. BOOTH—Mr. Moderator, I rise to a point of order.

Dr. BRIGGS—[Interposing] I have a right to reply to Col. McCook.

The MODERATOR—Let us hear what Dr. Booth's question of order is.

Dr. BOOTH—This Presbytery is assembled in obedience to the direction of the General Assembly, with a specific duty to perform. The General Assembly has decided, as we have heard, concerning the points that have been presented to us just now. We are therefore at this time obligated by the laws of order to proceed with the duty laid upon us by the Supreme Court of the Presbyterian Church of the United States of America—to proceed with the trial. That stands in the records of the General Assembly based upon a decision of all these questions that have been raised in the protest of Dr. Briggs. Now, sir, I ask for the decision of the Moderator as to whether anything is in order at this time except to proceed in compliance with the direction of the General Assembly with the trial of this case.

[Questions as to the roll interrupted the discussion for a few moments.]

The MODERATOR—Now, as to Dr. Booth's point of order which he raised——

Dr. BRIGGS—But before that point of order is decided, Mr. Moderator, I claim that I have a right as a party to reply.

The MODERATOR—You raised your objections and Col. McCook answered them.

Dr. CHARLES S. ROBINSON—Dr. Briggs has been out of order. That is Dr. Booth's point.

Dr. BRIGGS—I simply made my objections, and then an argument was presented on the other side, and I have a right to answer that argument. According to the Book I have a right to be heard, and I claim my right.

Dr. J. FORD SUTTON—A question of order is proper at any time, Mr. Moderator.

The MODERATOR—The point of order is raised by Dr. Booth that the question of raising these objections by Dr. Briggs at this time is out of order in view of the specific action of the General Assembly directing us now to take up this matter and act upon the sufficiency of the charges and specifications in form and legal effect. The Moderator decides that that point of order is well taken.

Dr. FRANCIS BROWN—May I call the attention of the Moderator to the Book of Discipline, which requires that "questions as to order or evidence, arising in the course of a trial, shall, after the parties have had an opportunity to be heard, be decided by the Moderator."

The MODERATOR—And the Moderator understands that the parties have now been heard.

Dr. BROWN—The parties have not been heard on that point of order.

Dr. BRIGGS—I claim that one party has been heard in argument against my objections, and I claim that I have a right as a party to be heard in argument in behalf of my objections, and to meet the argument of the other side before any further decision is made by the Moderator.

Dr. ROBINSON—I do not think it is understood clearly what Dr. Booth's point of order was. His point of order was this: that this discussion concerning who are the parties in this case has been decided by the General Assembly, and that it is out of order for us to do anything but obey the Supreme Court of our Church. That is what we are talking about in this whole discussion, as we say this is out of order from Dr. Briggs' beginning to Dr. Briggs' continuance. That is the question of order which we suppose the Moderator has now decided.

The MODERATOR—In view of the reminder of Dr.

Brown, the Moderator would recall his decision in order that the parties may be heard under the rule. It seems to be clear as a question of order that is now raised by Dr. Booth. Section 27 of the Book of Discipline provides as follows: " Questions as to order or evidence, arising in the course of a trial, shall, after the parties have had an opportunity to be heard, be decided by the Moderator, subject to appeal."

Dr. ROBINSON—Will the Moderator state who are the parties to be heard?

The MODERATOR—The parties are the Presbyterian Church in the United States of America as represented by this Prosecuting Committee on the one side, and Dr. Charles A. Briggs as the defendant, on the other side.

Dr. SUTTON—I submit that there is no question before the house but the point of order. It is the point of the order in which those brethren are to be heard, and nothing more. If Dr. Briggs has any remarks to make on the point of order he should be heard; but that is all.

Dr. BOOTH—Will the Moderator rule according to that statement and keep us to that law? It is the question of the point of order on which the parties are to be heard—not the subject-matter that has occasioned the presenting of the point of order.

Dr. BRIGGS—I wish to enter my solemn protest against the refusal of the Moderator to hear me as a party in response to the argument of this so-called Committee of Prosecution against my objection, when I expressly reserved the right to argue the case provided they argued it; and I shall include that in any complaint or appeal that I may hereafter be obliged to make to the Synod of New York.

The MODERATOR—The Moderator did not intend to prevent you from being heard in respect to the matter.

Dr. BRIGGS—But I understand that a decision on this point of order does rule me from the floor.

The MODERATOR—Yes, if the house so decides.

Dr. BRIGGS— Now, I shall speak to this point of order. I claim that according to Section 27 I not only have the right as a party to file objections to the charges and specifications as to their sufficiency, but I also have the right to make any other preliminary objections. I think you will see that clearly, that I have the right to make any other preliminary objections. Now, these I have brought specifically before you as preliminary objections which I, as a party, have a right to make. These objections are germane to the case. It is necessary for me to make them, as I endeavored to show you. It is claimed that the General Assembly has decided these questions. I deny it. I claim that the Synod of New York has forced me, whether I will or not, as an upright and honorable man, to raise this question before you, and I am simply doing my duty in raising the question before you, and I wish to have no argument upon it, as I said at the beginning, but simply a vote in order that either one way or the other it may be decided and be made a ground of appeal to the higher court, and you cannot prevent that. If you refuse to hear me I appeal against your decision not to hear me, and bring the whole case before them in that way.

Dr. BOOTH—Having raised the point of order, Mr. Moderator, am I not the party on the other side?

The MODERATOR—No, I think not.

Dr. BOOTH—On questions of order the parties are to be heard, and as I raise the question of order I am one of the parties.

Dr. JOHN J. STEVENSON—The defendant read a discussion of his objections, and after reading it he summed it up in a final paper, and so he gave his objections after the discussion. And now one point with reference to his statement. This Committee takes issue at once, finally and absolutely, with respect to the inference and value of that complaint——

Dr. BROWN—[Interposing] I rise to a question of order.

Dr. STEVENSON—I have the floor, sir.

Dr. BROWN—Mr. Moderator, I desire to inquire if this gentleman is speaking to the point of order before us?

The MODERATOR—The question of order is before us.

Dr. BROWN—I submit that brother Stevenson is not addressing himself to that.

Dr. STEVENSON—I shall endeavor to hold myself strictly to that question, sir. The defendant stated that he was compelled to take this position and present the preliminary objections by the action of the Synod of New York. The Synod of New York took no action whatever. It could take no action whatever with respect to this case in any shape or form, because this is a judicial case. There was nothing before it, except what purported to be a complaint in a form non-judicial. This case was never before the Synod in any form whatever. Consequently, the argument offered by the defendant on this point is without value in any way. These preliminary objections should have come in when he stated that he offered no objections to the authority of the Presbytery. He offered only his objections to the form and legal effect of the charges. That is all he offered.

The MODERATOR—The Moderator would prefer instead of seeming to limit Dr. Briggs, or to in any way lessen the liberty in the matter, to have him heard to a reasonable extent in setting forth the matter. He wishes that distinctly understood. It would seem that a full explanation had been had by Dr. Briggs, and then that was met by the rejoinder on the other side ; and, if the house would allow that, the Moderator would be very glad, rather than to insist upon a decision that might seem to exclude him.

Dr. BRIGGS—Did I understand that I am to speak, or not?

Dr. ROBINSON—What does Dr. Briggs want to do? I believe that there is not a man in this whole building that does not want to hear everything he has to say. Everybody's heart is in earnest in saying that. If I voice anything, I insist upon that statement. But is there never to be any end of the argument whether or not that Committee is a party? Having had it decided at the top of our whole church that the Committee was a party, it seemed to us that it was not necessary for him to discuss that particular again and again and again. I would be glad for one to hear Dr. Briggs on any point that he chooses to speak upon, but we are getting tired of the over-discussion of that which the General Assembly has decided.

The MODERATOR—Then, sir, the Moderator's decision is this: That in view of the action taken by the General Assembly upon the recommendation of the Judicial Committee, this whole subject having been fully discussed in that Committee——

Dr. BRIGGS—[Interrupting] Mr. Moderator, will you allow me one word? That has been argued by the other side, and I have had no opportunity of meeting that, and you are deciding on the basis of their argument.

The MODERATOR—The Moderator must make a decision, and he is simply trying to do so. This subject having been fully discussed in the Judicial Committee, and having been embodied in their report recommending the entertainment of the appeal to the General Assembly, also having been embodied in the minute which was presented by the General Assembly as its finding in this case, sending this case back to the Presbytery, and also finding voice in the protest on the part of the brethren who objected to the proceeding, and who embodied these principles as having been recognized by the action of the Assembly; and now, the matter coming before us in this single way, that we are to pass upon and determine the sufficiency of the charges and specifications in form and legal effect, my decision is that this is now out of order. The Moderator's decision is, of course, subject to appeal.

Dr. BROWN—I beg very respectfully to appeal from the decision of the Moderator on this question. It is not my desire or the desire of any of those who sympathize with Dr. Briggs, I am sure, to interpose any hindrance to our getting at the matter in hand directly, but it does seem unjust, if I may be allowed to say so, that action in other courts should by any interpretation be allowed to interfere with what seems to be the obvious right to have this fundamental question considered and decided. I beg to appeal from the decision of the Moderator.

Rev. CHARLES R. GILLETT—I second that.

The MODERATOR—Appeal is made from the Moderator's decision, that is, those who sustain the appeal will vote against this motion, and those not in favor of the appeal will sustain the Moderator's decision.

Dr. BOOTH—Nó, you are putting it the wrong way.

Dr. ROBINSON—The question should be: Shall the Moderator be sustained?

The MODERATOR—Strictly speaking, it is: Shall the appeal be sustained?

Dr. BOOTH—Shall the appeal be sustained? That is, shall Dr. Brown's appeal be sustained by the vote of this house? Those who desire to do so will vote in the affirmative. Those who desire to sustain the Moderator will vote in the negative.

Dr. VAN DYKE—I am reluctant as anybody, either to hear this question discussed, or to add one word——

Elder W. R. WORRALL—[Interrupting] If you will look in your Book of Discipline, Mr. Moderator, it provides that no debate shall be allowed on an appeal from the decision of the Moderator.

The MODERATOR—I would say that if Dr. Van Dyke wishes to debate the question, it is not debatable.

Elder WORRALL—Mr. Moderator, I ask for a decision on my point. There is no debate allowed on this question.

Dr. VAN DYKE—Yes, sir, there is. An appeal which involves a constitutional question is debatable, and this involves a constitutional question.

The MODERATOR—The Moderator must beg leave to differ with you, sir. It is to be decided by the Moderator, subject to appeal.

Dr. VAN DYKE—I am strongly of the impression, sir, that an appeal which involves a constitutional question is debatable. I wish to call attention to the fact that we are really passing upon this great constitutional question at this time in this vote.

Elder WORRALL—I call the speaker to order.

The MODERATOR—The Presbytery will understand from what Dr. Van Dyke has said that we are virtually deciding what is called a constitutional question. The Moderator is obliged to make a decision under the point of order, and he would not be understood as assuming any authority in the matter, but only as acting as according to the rules of the book as far as they can be understood. Now, the appeal is from the decision of the Moderator.

Dr. ROBINSON—What is that constitutional question? [Cries of Question! Question!]

The MODERATOR—One moment, brethren. The constitutional question is as to the status of the Committee.

Dr. ROBINSON—No, sir, I beg your pardon. I supposed the Moderator had the wrong idea of that, and that is the reason I arose. The question that was put to the Moderator was whether, when the Supreme Court of our Church had decided it, a further discussion of it was becoming and in order here in this Presbytery. That is the question.

[Calls were again made for the question.]

Brethren need not call upon me to stop, or call for the question. I want to know what the constitutional question is, and that is whether, when the General Assembly has decided the question, we have any reason further to debate who the parties to it are. That is the question from which appeal is taken.

The MODERATOR—The Moderator understood that the constitutional question, in the first place, applied to the status of the Committee, and then that Dr. Van Dyke's point involved a constitutional question as to our right to discuss the appeal.

Dr. BROWN—Am I right in understanding that the question as to whether the Assembly has decided the matter in such a way as to preclude discussion here is really involved in the ruling of the Moderator?

The MODERATOR—It is involved so far that the highest court of the Church, having taken that action, that carries this question with it; and now, in view of all that, we have the case brought before us with that action back of it, that therefore it is not in order that the question should be raised here.

Dr. BROWN—It is the ruling of the Moderator, in effect, that the Assembly has in such a way decided that it is not in order here to raise the question. It is, then, the understanding of the Moderator that the effect of an appeal from that decision is to bring out a difference of opinion, if there be such in the Presbytery, as to whether the action of the Assembly does carry that effect with it? That is my understanding of the appeal.

The MODERATOR—Yes, sir. Of course it is a question as to the mind of the body, and the Moderator is very glad to have the whole body express its opinion in that way and to share the responsibility of it.

Dr. BROWN—Those, then, that find themselves compelled to vote against the Moderator, are to be understood not as voting against the General Assembly?

Elder WORRALL—I shall insist upon my point of order, that this debate is out of order.

Dr. BROWN—My desire is simply to get an understanding of how we are to vote.

Elder WORRALL—I insist upon my point of order.

The MODERATOR—Give Dr. Brown an opportunity to make his statement. It is not polite to interrupt him.

Dr. BROWN—I wish to know whether I am right in supposing that those who vote to sustain the Moderator——

Dr. SUTTON—[Interrupting] It matters not what Dr. Brown understands or supposes about the Moderator one way or another. The Moderator has decided a plain open question, and Dr. Brown or anybody else may place such construction upon it afterwards as they choose as a basis of complaint and of appeal; but the

Moderator has decided, and therefore the question before us is: Shall the Moderator be sustained or not?

Dr. BROWN—But the Moderator had already expressed himself as thinking it wise that the house should fully understand what was involved in the ruling, and that is all I wished to bring up; and I think in voting against the Moderator—and we will all do it with regret, I am sure—that we are simply expressing our opinion that the Assembly has not decided in the way indicated.

[Cries of Question! Question!]

The MODERATOR—Brethren, the appeal is before you.

Dr. BRIGGS—As it may be necessary to appeal to the higher courts, I would like to have the decision of the Moderator read before action is taken.

The MODERATOR—Very well.

Dr. HENRY M. FIELD—Dr. Parkhurst and myself do not comprehend what the question is. We had an instance once before, you remember, when those who voted to sustain the Moderator did not know what it was they were voting on.

Elder WORRALL—Let the stenographer read the decision of the Moderator from his notes.

The MODERATOR—We want it perfectly clear in regard to the matter, and we want to know just what the points are, and then we can act intelligently. I have made a decision, and I will call upon the stenographer to read it so as to have it clear in the minds of all.

[The stenographer then read from his notes as follows]:

" That in view of the action taken by the General Assembly upon the recommendation of the Judicial Committee, this whole subject having been fully discussed in that Committee, and having been embodied in their report recommending the entertainment of the appeal to the General Assembly, also having been embodied in the minute which was presented by the General Assembly as its finding in this case, sending this case back to the Presbytery, and also finding voice in the protest on the part of the brethren who objected to the proceeding and who embodied these principles as having been recognized by the action of the Assembly; and now, the matter coming before us in this single way, that we are to pass upon and determine as to sufficiency of the charges and specifications in form and legal effect, my decision is that this is now out of order."

The MODERATOR—The question is on the appeal from that decision of the Moderator.

Dr. MARVIN R. VINCENT—Will the Chair state how we shall express our vote? I move that we vote in this way—to sustain the appeal, or not to sustain it.

The MODERATOR—I think that perhaps the better way would be to vote to sustain the decision of the Moderator, or not to sustain it. I think that will be clearer. If you are in favor of the decision of the Moderator you will vote against the appeal.

Dr. ROBINSON—An appeal is a motion. An appeal was taken from the decision of the Moderator, and it was seconded. Now, those that favor it will be against the decision of the Moderator.

Dr. BIRCH—There have been so many interruptions that I would ask the Moderator to state his decision over again without interruption, before we take this vote.

The MODERATOR—The decision of the Moderator is this——

Dr. BRIGGS—[Interposing] Are we going to stand on the previous decision, or on the one you are going to make now?

The MODERATOR—I will try to make the same one over again, sir, and then we will have to let one or the other stand as my decision. The decision of the Moderator is this: That this question as to the status of the Prosecuting Committee, having been met and fully discussed in the Judicial Committee, and having been embodied in its report finding the appeal in order and recommending the entertainment of the appeal, and that report having been adopted by the Assembly, and the appeal having thus been sustained, and the minute which was brought in as a finding of the action of the General Assembly in the case, and also the protest that was made on the floor of the Assembly by those who opposed its action, which protest was based upon the recognition of the principles that are involved as to the status of the Committee, its power and province—that protest embodying these things—I decide that the matter now coming back to us upon the recommendation of the General Assembly, that we shall now pass upon and determine the sufficiency of the charges and specifications in form and in legal effect, that thing singly being before us, this is out of order.*

---

* In the Minutes of Presbytery, the Moderator's ruling is given as follows: "That the raising of the question of the status of the Prosecuting Committee and of its right to appear and continue the conduct of this case is not now in order, for these reasons:

" 1st. That this whole question was fully discussed and decided by the Judicial Committee of the General Assembly.

" 2nd. That the recognition of the status of the Committee and its powers as defined in the appeal were embodied in the Judicial Committee's report recommending the entertainment of the appeal.

" 3rd. That in the minute of the General Assembly giving its finding in the case, the Committee's status is clearly recognized.

" 4th. That the protest recorded in the Minutes of the General Assembly by those objecting to its action was based on the fact that its action in entertaining the appeal gave the Committee the standing and powers claimed for it; and

" Lastly. That the order sending the case again to this Presbytery, requiring

Dr. ALBERT B. KING—Dr. Brown appealed from your decision. Will the vote be upon the appeal?

The MODERATOR—Those in favor of the appeal are against the Moderator, and those who are not in favor of the appeal are in favor of the Moderator's decision. Those in favor of sustaining this appeal will say aye; opposed, no.

[A *viva voce* vote was then taken.]

The MODERATOR—The Moderator decides that the noes have it.

Dr. BROWN—I call for a division.

The MODERATOR—A division is called for. Those in favor of sustaining the appeal and against the Moderator's decision will rise.

[58 arose.]

Those against sustaining the appeal and in favor of the Moderator's decision will now rise.

[73 arose.]

The MODERATOR—The decision of the Moderator is sustained by a vote of 73 to 58.

Dr. BRIGGS—I beg to give notice of appeal and complaint to the Synod against this decision of the Presbytery.

C. *Complaint to the Synod of New York, against the Presbytery of New York, for Action taken November 9th, 1892.*

NEW YORK, November 18, 1892.

Complaint is hereby made before the Synod of New York, by the persons whose names are appended below, being all of them persons subject and submitting to the

---

us to proceed to pass upon and determine the sufficiency of the Charges and Specifications, as to form and legal effect, and to proceed with the trial—this being the single point before us to be acted upon, therefore the Moderator's decision is that this question is out of order."

jurisdiction of the Presbytery of New York, in accordance with Sections 83 and 86 of the Revised Book of Discipline, against the action of the Presbytery of New York, November 9th, 1892, in sustaining by a vote of 73 to 58 the ruling of the Moderator, as follows:

"That the raising of the question of the status of the Prosecuting Committee [in the case of the Rev. Charles A. Briggs, D.D.], and of its right to appear and continue the conduct of this case, is not now in order."

Against this action, complaint is made for the following reasons:

1. The case having been remanded to the Presbytery by the General Assembly "for a new trial" [Minutes, 1892, p. 152], it was competent for the defendant, according to Section 22 of the Revised Book of Discipline, to file "any substantial objection affecting the order or regularity of the proceeding," and "the raising of the question of the status of the Prosecuting Committee" was such an objection. To rule this objection out of order deprived the defendant of his right, under the action of the Assembly.

2. The Synod of New York in effect authorized the raising of this objection, when, in declining, October 21, 1892, to act on a complaint dealing with the same question, it gave as a reason for its decision the following: "First, The case, through the action of the General Assembly and of the Presbytery of New York, is again before the Presbytery, and the complainants may there have their remedy in their own hands."

3. The Moderator had been requested by the defendant to appoint a time for the offering of the said objection, and had appointed the time at which the objection was actually presented and filed, and at which he sub-

sequently declared it to be out of order; and no exception had been taken by any member of the Presbytery to this appointment.

4. The defendant submitted his objection without argument, reserving the right to argue, if argument should be made by the opposing party. Such argument was in fact made, and the defendant rose to reply, but was refused the floor and deprived of the opportunity of defending his objection by the Moderator's decision on the said question of order.

5. The Moderator, by his ruling, in effect passed upon the objection of the defendant, instead of giving the judicatory the opportunity to decide, according to section 22 of the Revised Book of Discipline.

6. The Moderator's reasons for his decision were insufficient, as follows:

(*a*). The statement " 1st, That this whole question was fully discussed and decided by the Judicial Committee of the General Assembly " is an insufficient reason, because no decision of a Judicial Committee can as such be of authority in the church, and binding on a Presbytery.

(*b*). The statement " 2nd, That the recognition of the status of the Committee and its powers as defined in the appeal were embodied in the Judicial Committee's report recommending the entertainment of the appeal " is an in- sufficient reason, because it does not appear that the Assembly adopted that part of the report of its Judicial Committee which contained " the recognition of the status of the Committee and its powers as defined in the appeal."

(*c*). The statement " 3rd, That in the minute of the General Assembly giving its finding in the case, the Committee's status is clearly recognized," is an insufficient reason, because the Committee's status is recognized in this finding only by indirection, it is assumed and not decided. The Committee appeared before the Assembly with the Presbytery's action of November 4, 1891, behind them, and were received as, *prima facie*, in good standing, the question as to their standing not being before the Assembly, and the Assembly not being legally competent to consider and pass upon it.

(*d*). The statement " 4th, That the Protest recorded in the Minutes of the General Assembly by those objecting to its action was based on the fact that its action in entertaining the appeal gave the Committee the standing and powers claimed for it " is an insufficient reason, because the Presbytery was in no way bound by the act or opinion of individual members of the Assembly.

(*e*). The statement " Lastly, That the order sending the case again to this Presbytery, requiring us to proceed to pass upon and determine the sufficiency of the charges and specifications, as to form and legal effect, and to proceed with the trial—this being the single point before us to be acted upon " is an insufficient reason, because it misstates the action of the Assembly and also draws a false inference from the action of the Assembly.

(1). It misstates the action of the Assembly, which was as follows: " The General Assembly having on the 28th day of May, 1892, duly sustained all of the specifications of error alleged and set forth in the appeal and specifications in this case, it is now, May 30th, 1892, ordered that the judgment of the Presbytery of New York, entered November 4th, 1891, dismissing the case of the Presbyterian Church in the United States of America against Rev. Charles A. Briggs, D.D., be, and the same is hereby reversed, and the case is remanded to the Presbytery of New York for a new trial, with directions to said Presbytery to proceed to pass upon and determine the sufficiency of the charges and specifications in form and legal effect, and to permit the prosecuting committee to amend the specifications or charges, not changing the general nature of the same, if, in the furtherance of justice, it be necessary to amend, so that the case may be brought to issue and tried on the merits thereof as speedily as may be practicable."

(2). It also draws a false inference from the action of the Assembly, viz., that the single point to be acted upon was the sufficiency of the charges presented October 5th, 1891, in form and legal effect, whereas the evident purpose of the Assembly was not to prescribe the exact order of procedure in the Presbytery, but to secure a definite decision of the Presbytery on the sufficiency of the charges and specifications. In fact, the Presbytery did not, after the Moderator's ruling, follow the exact order of procedure named above, and did not pass upon the charges and specifications aforesaid, but permitted the Committee at once to bring in amended charges, and in so doing were led and encouraged by the Moderator himself, who said: "It would save the time of the House if we do not stand upon the literal reading of this mandate." [Stenographer's Report, pp. 63, 64].

7. The points of objection which were filed by the defendant and the consideration of which was ruled out of order, were in fact substantial and weighty objections, as follows:

"(1). A Committee originally appointed to 'arrange and prepare the necessary proceedings appropriate in the case of Dr. Briggs' appears before you claiming to be a committee of prosecution, and they are recognized as such by the Moderator's giving them the floor to act in that capacity. But their right so to act is legally questioned by complaint to the Synod of New York, and it has not yet been lawfully determined by the Synod.

"(2). This Committee appeared before the General Assembly as an original party, and acted as such by presenting an appeal against the judgment of the Presbytery in dismissing the case against me. They now appear before you as an original party successful in their appeal. Their right to act as an original party is questioned in the said complaint, and it has not yet been lawfully determined by the Synod.

"(3). This Committee claim to represent the Presbyterian Church in the United States of America, and to be independent of this Presbytery which appointed them. They acted independently of the Presbytery by appealing to the General Assembly against the judgment of the Presbytery in dismissing the case against me. They now appear before you with a reversal of the judgment of the Presbytery which they have obtained. Their right to act independently of the Presbytery is questioned in the said complaint, and it has not yet been lawfully determined by the Synod.

"(4). This Committee appear before you having acted, as is claimed, in violation of the constitution of the Church, which provides that when a complaint has been signed by more than one-third of those present and voting in the Presbytery it acts as a stay to further proceedings. The above mentioned complaint signed by a majority of the voters, has been filed with the Synod of New York, and is now in the possession of the Synod. Until the questions raised in said Complaint have been determined, this Committee cannot legally take any action in the matters complained of. They cannot act as a prosecuting committee, or as an original party, or as independent of the Presbytery; and you cannot allow them so to act without a violation of the law of complaint embedded in the constitution of the Church."

8. The Committee had in fact no right to act as a committee of prosecution under Section 11 of the Revised Book of Discipline, because the records of the Presbytery do not show that it was appointed as such.

9. The Committee had in fact no right to appear as an original party, because, according to Section 10 of the Revised Book of Discipline, "When the prosecution is initiated by a judicatory the Presbyterian Church in the United States of America shall be the prosecutor, and an original party": but the Presbyterian Church in the United States of America was represented in the house by the Presbytery of New York itself, and not by a committee of the Presbytery.

10. The Committee had in fact no right to act inde-pendently of the Presbytery by appealing to the General Assembly, and securing a reversal of the decision of the Presbytery, November 4, 1891, dismissing the case against Dr. Briggs, because every committee appointed by Presbytery is subject to the control of Presbytery, otherwise the creature is greater than the body creating it, the sovereignty of Presbytery over its members, its committees and all the interests committed to it by the laws of the Church is seriously impaired, and an undue power is placed in the hands of a few persons.

11. The question raised as a point of order and de-cided by the Moderator was in fact one of law and juris-diction, and as such its decision belonged not to the Moderator, but to the judicatory itself, after due consid-eration. Hence the Moderator had no right to make the decision, and the Presbytery had no right to sustain him on appeal.

For these reasons, and in view of the fact that the

Synod of New York adopted and gave the following decision, October 21, 1892, *viz.:*

"In the matter of Judicial Case Number 3 the committee find the Complaint to be in order, but recommend that it is inexpedient to take action at the present time, for the following reasons:

"First. The case, through the action of the General Assembly and of the Presbytery of New York, is again before the Presbytery, and the complainants may there have their remedy in their own hands.

"Second. In case the remedy there be found insufficient, they will afterward have opportunity, by appeal or complaint to bring the case again before Synod";—
—and of the further fact, that the defendant, in accordance with the above decision, respectfully requested the Presbytery "to apply the said remedy, and in accordance with the provision of the Book of Discipline, to determine these preliminary objections," and of the further fact, that "the remedy there" has been "found insufficient," due notice of complaint having been given to the stated clerk of the Presbytery of New York, within ten days after the action complained of, according to section 84 of the Revised Book of Discipline, complaint is hereby made in due form to the next higher judicatory, being the Synod of New York, against the said action of the Presbytery of New York, and the Synod is most respectfully and earnestly requested to entertain this Complaint, and to take therein such action as shall in its judgment appear wise and likely to promote good order, justice, and the peace, purity, and welfare of the Church of Christ.

[Signed],   C. A. BRIGGS,
              FRANCIS BROWN,
                    etc., etc.
[Here follows a list of names.]

II.

CHARGE I.

The Presbyterian Church in the United States of America charges the Rev. Charles A. Briggs, D.D., being a Minister of the said Church and a member of the Presbytery of New York, with teaching that the Reason is a fountain of divine authority which may and does savingly enlighten men, even such men as reject the Scriptures as the authoritative proclamation of the will of God, and reject also the way of salvation through the mediation and sacrifice of the Son of God as revealed therein; which is contrary to the essential doctrine of the Holy Scripture and of the Standards of the said Church, that the Holy Scripture is most necessary, and the rule of faith and practice.

SPECIFICATION I.

In an Inaugural Address, which the said Rev. Charles A. Briggs, D.D., delivered at the Union Theological Seminary in the city of New York, January 20th, 1891, on the occasion of his induction into the Edward Robinson Chair of Biblical Theology, which Address has been published and extensively circulated with the knowledge and approval of the said Rev. Charles A. Briggs, D.D., and has been republished by him in a second edition with a preface and an appendix, there occur the following sentences:

Page 24, lines 7–10 and 31–33:

"Divine authority is the only authority to which man can yield implicit obedience, on which he can rest in loving certainty and build with joyous confidence. . . . . There are historically three great fountains of divine authority—the Bible, the Church, and the Reason."

Page 27, lines 9–21:

"Martineau could not find divine authority in the Church or the Bible. but he did find God enthroned in his own soul. There are those who would refuse these rationalists a place in the company of the faithful. But they forget that the essential thing is to find God and divine certainty, and if these men have found God without the mediation of Church and Bible, Church and Bible are means and not ends; they are avenues to God, but are not God. We regret that these rationalists depreciate the means of grace so essential to most of us, but we are warned lest we commit a similar error, and depreciate the reason and the Christian consciousness."

Inaugural Address, Appendix, Second Edition, pages 88, 89:

"(c). Unless God's authority is discerned in the forms of the Reason, there is no ground upon which any of the heathen could ever have been saved, for they know nothing of Bible or Church. If they are not savingly enlightened by the Light of the World in the forms of the Reason the whole heathen world is lost forever."

SPECIFICATION II.

In an Inaugural Address, which the said Rev. Charles A. Briggs, D.D., delivered at the Union Theological Seminary in the city of New York, January 20th, 1891, on the occasion of his induction into the Edward Robinson Chair of Biblical Theology, which Address has been published and extensively circulated with the knowledge and approval of the said Rev. Charles A. Briggs, D.D., and has been republished by him in a second edition with a preface and an appendix, there occur the following sentences:

Page 28, lines 1 to 22:

"(3). *The Authority of Holy Scripture.*—We have examined the Church and the Reason as seats of divine authority in an introduction to our theme, *the Authority of the Scriptures*, because they open our eyes to see mistakes that are common to the three departments. Protestant Christianity builds its faith and life on the divine authority contained in the Scriptures, and too often depreciates the Church and the Reason. Spurgeon is an example of the average modern Evangelical, who holds the Protestant position, and assails the Church and Reason in the interest of the authority of Scripture. But the average opinion of the Christian world would not assign him a higher place in the kingdom of God than Martineau or Newman. May we not conclude, on the whole, that these three representative Christians of our time, living in or near the world's metropolis, have, each in his way, found God and rested on divine authority? May we not learn from them not to depreciate any of the means whereby God makes himself known to men? Men are influenced by their temperaments and environments which of the three ways of access to God they may pursue."

These declarations are contrary to Scripture:

Isaiah viii. 20; Matt. x. 32, 33; Luke xvi. 29–31; John v. 39; xiv. 6; 1 John v. 10; Gal. i. 9; 2 Timothy iii. 15–17; 2 Peter i. 19–21.

These declarations are contrary to the Standards:
Confession of Faith, Chap I., Secs. I., V., VI., X.
Larger Catechism, Q. 2, 3.   Shorter Catechism, Q. 2.

CHARGE II.

The Presbyterian Church in the United States of
America charges the Rev. Charles A. Briggs, D.D., being a Minister of the said Church and a member of the
Presbytery of New York, with teaching that the Church
is a fountain of divine authority which, apart from the
Holy Scripture, may and does savingly enlighten men ;
which is contrary to the essential doctrine of the Holy
Scripture and of the Standards of the said Church, that
the Holy Scripture is most necessary and the rule of
faith and practice.

SPECIFICATION I.

In an Inaugural Address, which the said Rev. Charles
A. Briggs, D.D., delivered at the Union Theological
Seminary in the City of New York, January 20th, 1891,
on the occasion of his induction into the Edward Robinson Chair of Biblical Theology, which Address has been
published and extensively circulated with the knowledge and approval of the said Rev. Charles A. Briggs,
D.D., and has been republished by him in a second edition with a preface and an appendix, there occur the
following sentences:

Page 24, lines 7–10 and 31–33 :

" Divine authority is the only authority to which man
can yield implicit obedience, on which he can rest in loving certainty and build with joyous confidence. . . . . .
There are historically three great fountains of divine
authority—the Bible, the Church, and the Reason."

Page 25, lines 1 to 14 inclusive:

"(1.) *The Authority of the Church.*—The majority of Christians from the apostolic age have found God through the Church. Martyrs and Saints, Fathers and Schoolmen, the profoundest intellects, the saintliest lives, have had this experience. Institutional Christianity has been to them the presence-chamber of God. They have therein and thereby entered into communion with all saints. It is difficult for many Protestants to regard this experience as any other than pious illusion and delusion. But what shall we say of a modern like Newman, who could not reach certainty, striving never so hard, through the Bible or the Reason, but who did find divine authority in the institutions of the Church?"

SPECIFICATION II.

In an Inaugural Address, which the said Rev. Charles A. Briggs, D.D., delivered at the Union Theological Seminary in the City of New York, January 20th, 1891, on the occasion of his induction into the Edward Robinson Chair of Biblical Theology, which Address has been published and extensively circulated with the knowledge and approval of the said Rev. Charles A. Briggs, D.D., and has been republished by him in a second edition with a preface and an appendix, there occur the following sentences:

Page 28, lines 1 to 22, are:

"(3.) *The Authority of Holy Scripture.*—We have examined the Church and the Reason as seats of divine authority in an introduction to our theme, the *Authority of the Scriptures*, because they open our eyes to see mistakes that are common to the three departments. Protestant Christianity builds its faith and life on the divine authority contained in the Scriptures, and too often de-

preciates the Church and the Reason. Spurgeon is an
example of the average modern Evangelical, who holds
the Protestant position, and assails the Church and
Reason in the interest of the authority of Scripture.
But the average opinion of the Christian world would
not assign him a higher place in the kingdom of God
than Martineau or Newman. May we not conclude, on
the whole, that these three representative Christians of
our time, living in or near the world's metropolis, have,
each in his way, found God and rested on divine authority? May we not learn from them not to depreciate
any of the means whereby God makes himself known to
men? Men are influenced by their temperaments and
environments which of the three ways of access to God
they may pursue."

These declarations are contrary to the Holy Scripture:

Isaiah viii. 20; Matt. x. 32, 33; Luke xvi. 29–31;
John v. 39; xiv. 6; 1 John v. 10; Gal. i. 9; 2 Timothy
iii. 15–17; 2 Peter i. 19–21.

These declarations are contrary to the Standards:

Confession of Faith, Chap. I., Secs. I., V., VI., X.

Larger Catechism, Q. 2, 3.   Shorter Catechism, Q. 2.

CHARGE III.

The Presbyterian Church in the United States of
America charges the Rev. Charles A. Briggs, D.D.,
being a Minister of the said Church and a member of
the Presbytery of New York, with teaching that errors
may have existed in the original text of the Holy Scripture, as it came from its authors, which is contrary to
the essential doctrine taught in the Holy Scripture and
in the Standards of the said Church, that the Holy

Scripture is the Word of God written, immediately in-spired, and the rule of faith and practice.

In an Inaugural Address, which the said Rev. Charles A. Briggs, D.D., delivered at the Union Theological Seminary in the City of New York, January 20th, 1891, on the occasion of his induction into the Edward Robin-son Chair of Biblical Theology, which Address has been published and extensively circulated with the knowledge and approval of the said Rev. Charles A. Briggs, D.D., and has been republished by him in a second edition with a preface and an appendix, there occur the follow-ing sentences, beginning with line 4 of page 35 :

" I shall venture to affirm that, so far as I can see, there are errors in the Scriptures that no one has been able to explain away ; and the theory that they were not in the original text is sheer assumption, upon which no mind can rest with certainty. If such errors destroy the authority of the Bible, it is already destroyed for historians. Men cannot shut their eyes to truth and fact. But on what authority do these theologians drive men from the Bible by this theory of inerrancy? The Bible itself nowhere makes this claim. The creeds of the Church nowhere sanction it. It is a ghost of modern evangelicalism to frighten children. The Bible has maintained its authority with the best scholars of our time, who with open minds have been willing to recog-nize any error that might be pointed out by Historical Criticism ; for these errors are all in the circumstantials and not in the essentials ; they are in the human setting, not in the precious jewel itself ; they are found in that section of the Bible that theologians commonly account for from the providential superintendence of the mind of the author, as distinguished from divine revelation itself. It may be that this providential superintendence gives infallible guidance in every particular; and it may be that it differs but little, if at all, from the providential superintendence of the fathers and schoolmen and theologians of the Christian Church. It is not important for our purpose that we should decide this question. If we should abandon the whole field of providential superintendence so far as inspiration and divine authority are concerned and limit divine inspiration and authority to the essential contents of the Bible, to its religion, faith, and morals, we would still have ample room to seek divine authority where alone it is essential, or even important, in the teaching that guides our devotions, our thinking, and our conduct."

These declarations are contrary to the statements of Scripture:

Zech. vii. 12; Mark vii. 13; Romans iii. 1, 2; 1 Cor. ii. 13; Galatians iii. 8; 2 Pet. i. 20, 21; 2 Tim. iii. 16.

These statements are contrary to the Standards:

Confession of Faith, Chap. I., Secs. I., II., IV., VIII.

CHARGE IV.

The Presbyterian Church in the United States of America charges the Rev. Charles A. Briggs, D.D., being a Minister in said Church and a member of the Presbytery of New York, with teaching that many of the Old Testament predictions have been reversed by history, and that the great body of Messianic prediction has not been and cannot be fulfilled, which is contrary to the essential doctrine of Holy Scripture and of the Standards of the said Church, that God is true, omniscient, and unchangeable.

SPECIFICATION.

In an Inaugural Address, which the said Rev. Charles A. Briggs, D.D., delivered at the Union Theological Seminary in the City of New York, January 20th, 1891, on the occasion of his induction into the Edward Robinson Chair of Biblical Theology, which Address has been published and extensively circulated with the knowledge and approval of the said Rev. Charles A. Briggs, D.D., and has been republished by him in a second edition with a preface and an appendix, there occur the following sentences:

Page 38, lines 20 to 30:

"(6.) *Minute Prediction.*—Another barrier to the Bible has been the interpretation put upon *Predictive Prophecy*, making it a sort of history before the time, and looking anxiously for the fulfillment of the details of Biblical prediction.   Kuenen has shown that if we insist upon the fulfillment of the details of the predictive prophecy of the Old Testament, many of these predictions have been reversed by history; and the great body of the Messianic prediction has not only never been fulfilled, but cannot now be fulfilled, for the reason that its own time has passed forever."

This declaration is contrary to Scripture:

Matt. v. 17, 18; xxiv. 15; Dan. xii. 11; Luke xxiv. 44; Exodus xxxiv. 6; Hebrews iv. 13; James i. 17.

This declaration is contrary to the Standards:

Confession of Faith, Chap. I., Section IV.; Chap. II., Secs. I., II.

Shorter Catechism, Q. 4.

Charge V.

The Presbyterian Church in the United States of America charges the Rev. Charles A. Briggs, D.D., being a Minister of the said Church and a member of the Presbytery of New York, with teaching that Moses is not the author of the Pentateuch, which is contrary to direct statements of Holy Scripture and to the essential doctrines of the Standards of the said Church, that the Holy Scripture evidences itself to be the word of God by the consent of all the parts, and that the infallible rule of interpretation of Scripture is the Scripture itself.

SPECIFICATION.

In an Inaugural Address, which the said Rev. Charles A. Briggs, D.D., delivered at the Union Theological Seminary in the City of New York, January 20th, 1891, on the occasion of his induction into the Edward Robinson Chair of Biblical Theology, which Address has been published and extensively circulated with the knowledge and approval of the said Rev. Charles A. Briggs, D.D., and has been republished by him in a second edition with a preface and an appendix, there occurs the following sentence:

Page 33, lines 6–8 :

"It may be regarded as the certain result of the science of the Higher Criticism that Moses did not write the Pentateuch."

This declaration is contrary to direct statements of Scripture :

Ex. xxiv. 4; Num. xxxiii. 2; Deut. v. 31; xxxi. 9; Josh. i. 7, 8; 1 Kings ii. 3; 1 Chron. vi. 49; Ezra iii. 2; vi. 18; Neh. i. 7; Luke xxiv. 27, 44; John v. 45–47; Acts vii. 38; xv. 21.

This declaration is contrary to the Standards:

Confession of Faith, Chap. I., Secs. V. and IX.

CHARGE VI.

The Presbyterian Church in the United States of America charges the Rev. Charles A. Briggs, D.D., being a Minister of the said Church and a member of the Presbytery of New York, with teaching that Isaiah is not the author of half of the book that bears his name, which is contrary to direct statements of Holy Scripture and to the essential doctrines of the Standards of the said Church that the Holy Scripture evidences itself to be the Word of God by the consent of all the parts, and that the infallible rule of interpretation of Scripture is the Scripture itself.

SPECIFICATION.

In an Inaugural Address, which the said Rev. Charles A. Briggs, D.D., delivered at the Union Theological Seminary in the City of New York, January 20th, 1891, on the occasion of his induction into the Edward Robinson Chair of Biblical Theology, which Address has been published and extensively circulated with the knowledge and approval of the said Rev. Charles A. Briggs, D.D., and has been republished by him in a second edition with a preface and an appendix, there occurs the following sentence:

Page 33, lines 14–15:

"Isaiah did not write half of the book that bears his name."

This declaration is contrary to direct statements of Scripture:

Matt. iv. 14, 15; xii. 17, 18; Luke iii. 4; Acts xxviii. 25, 26; John xii. 38, 41; Rom. x. 16, 20.

This declaration is contrary to the Standards:

Confession of Faith, Chap. I., Secs. V. and IX.

CHARGE VII.

The Presbyterian Church in the United States of America charges the Rev. Charles A. Briggs, D.D., being a Minister of said Church, and a member of the Presbytery of New York, with teaching that the processes of redemption extend to the world to come in the case of many who die in sin; which is contrary to the essential doctrine of Holy Scripture and the Standards of the said Church, that the processes of redemption are limited to this world.

SPECIFICATION.

In an Inaugural Address, which the said Rev. Charles A. Briggs, D.D., delivered at the Union Theological Seminary in the City of New York, January 20th, 1891, on the occasion of his induction into the Edward Robinson Chair of Biblical Theology, which Address has been published and extensively circulated with the knowledge and approval of the said Rev. Charles A. Briggs, D.D., and has been republished by him in a second edition with a preface and an appendix, there occur the following sentences:

Page 50: "The processes of redemption ever keep the *race* in mind. The Bible tells us of a race origin, a race sin, a race ideal, a race Redeemer, and a race redemption."

Page 53: "(*c.*) Another fault of Protestant theology is in its limitation of the process of redemption to this world, and its neglect of those vast periods of time which have elapsed for most men in the Middle State between death and the resurrection."

Pages 55 and 56: "The Bible does not teach universal salvation, but it does teach the salvation of the world, of the race of man, and that cannot be accomplished by the selection of a limited number of individuals from the mass. The holy arm that worketh salvation does not contract its hand in grasping only a few; it stretches its loving fingers so as to comprehend as many as possible—a definite number, but multitudes that no one can number. The salvation of the world can only mean the world as a whole, compared with which the unredeemed will be so few and insignificant, and evidently beyond the reach of redemption by their own act of rejecting it and hardening themselves against it, and by descending into such depths of demoniacal depravity in the Middle State, that they will vanish from the sight of the redeemed as altogether and irredeemably evil, and never more disturb the harmonies of the saints."

Inaugural Address, Appendix, 2d ed.

Page 104. This raises the question whether any man is irretrievably lost ere he commits this unpardonable sin, and whether those who do not commit it in this world ere they die are, by the mere crisis of death, brought into an unpardonable state; and whether, when Jesus said that this sin against the Holy Spirit was unpardonable here and also hereafter, he did not imply that all other sins might be pardoned hereafter as well as here.

These declarations are contrary to direct statements of Scripture:

Prov. xi. 7; Luke xvi. 22, 23; John viii. 24; 2 Cor. vi. 2; Heb. iv. 7.

These declarations are contrary to the Standards:

Confession of Faith, Chap. XXXII., Sec. I.

Larger Catechism, Q. 83, 86.

CHARGE VIII.

The Presbyterian Church in the United States of America charges the Rev. Charles A. Briggs, D.D., being a Minister of the said Church and a member of the Presbytery of New York, with teaching that Sanctification is not complete at death, which is contrary to the essential doctrine of Holy Scripture and of the Standards of the said Church that the souls of believers are at their death at once made perfect in holiness.

SPECIFICATION.

In an Inaugural Address, which the said Rev. Charles A. Briggs, D.D., delivered at the Union Theological Seminary in the City of New York, January 20th, 1891, on the occasion of his induction into the Edward Robinson Chair of Biblical Theology, which Address has been published and extensively circulated with the knowledge and approval of the said Rev. Charles A. Briggs, D.D., and has been republished by him in a second edition with a preface and an appendix, there occur the following sentences:

Pages 53, 54, 55:

"(c.) Another fault of Protestant theology is in its limitation of the process of redemption to this world, and its neglect of those vast periods of time which have elapsed for most men in the Middle State between death and the resurrection. The Roman Catholic Church is firmer here, though it smears the Biblical doctrine with not a few hurtful errors. The reaction against this limitation, as seen in the theory of second probation, is not surprising. I do not find this doctrine in the Bible, but I do find in the Bible the doctrine of a Middle State of conscious higher life in the communion with

Chiist and the multitude of the departed of all ages; and of the necessity of entire sanctification, in order that the work of redemption may be completed. There is no authority in the Scriptures, or in the creeds of Christendom, for the doctrine of immediate sanctification at death. The only sanctification known to experience, to Christian orthodoxy, and to the Bible, is progressive sanctification. Progressive sanctification after death, is the doctrine of the Bible and the Church; and it is of vast importance in our times that we should understand it, and live in accordance with it. The bugbear of a judgment immediately after death, and the illusion of a magical transformation in the dying hour, should be banished from the world. They are conceits derived from the Ethnic religions, and without basis in the Bible or Christian experience as expressed in the symbols of the Church. The former makes death a terror to the best of men, the latter makes human life and experience of no effect; and both cut the nerves of Christian activity and striving after sanctification. Renouncing them as hurtful, unchristian errors, we look with hope and joy for the continuation of the processes of grace, and the wonders of redemption in the company of the blessed, to which the faithful are all hastening."

Inaugural Address, Appendix, 2d ed., pages 107, 108, "Sanctification has two sides—a negative and a positive —mortification and vivification; the former is manward, the latter is Godward. Believers who enter the middle state, enter guiltless; they are pardoned and justified; they are mantled in the blood and righteousness of Christ; and nothing will be able to separate them from His love. They are also delivered from all temptations such as spring from without, from the world and the devil. They are encircled with influences for good such as they have never enjoyed before. But they are still the same persons, with all the gifts and graces, and also the same habits of mind, disposition, and temper they had when they left the world. Death destroys the body. It does not change the moral and religious nature of man. It is unpsychological and unethical to suppose that the character of the disembodied spirit will all be changed in the moment of death. It is the Manichean heresy to hold that sin belongs to the physical organization and is laid aside with the body. If this were so, how can any of our race carry their evil natures with them into the middle state and incur the punishment of their sins? The eternal punishment of a man whose evil nature has been stripped from him by death and left in the grave, is an absurdity. The Plymouth Brethren hold that there are two natures in the redeemed —the old man and the new. In accordance with such a theory, the old man might be cast off at death. But this is only a more subtle kind of Manicheism, which has ever been regarded as heretical. Sin, as our Saviour teaches, has its source in the heart—in the higher and immortal part of man. It is the work of sanctification to overcome sin in the higher nature."

These declarations are contrary to Scripture:

1 Cor. xv. 51, 52; Heb. xii. 23.

These declarations are contrary to the Standards:

Confession of Faith, Chap. XXXII., Sec. I.

Larger Catechism, Q. 86. Shorter Catechism, Q. 37.

The Presbyterian Church in the United States of America, represented by the undersigned Prosecuting Committee, offers in evidence the whole of the said Inaugural Address, both the first and second editions, and all the works of the said Rev. Charles A. Briggs, D.D., quoted therein, in so far as they bear upon this case; also the appendix to the second edition of said Address, and all the works of the said Rev. Charles A. Briggs, D.D., quoted therein, in so far as they bear upon this case; the whole of the Holy Scriptures and the whole of the Standards of the Presbyterian Church in the United States of America.

GEORGE W. F. BIRCH, D.D,.
JOSEPH J. LAMPE, D.D.,
ROBERT F. SAMPLE, D.D.,
JOHN J. STEVENSON,
JOHN J. McCOOK,
Prosecuting Committee.

III.

PRELIMINARY OBJECTIONS TO THE AMENDED CHARGES.

Mr. Moderator, Ministers and Elders of the Presbytery of New York:

I appear before you in compliance with your citation dated November 9th, 1892, to plead to the Amended Charges and Specifications placed in my hands by the Presbytery, on that date. The Book of Discipline, § 22, orders that "At the meeting at which the citations are returnable, the accused shall appear. He may file objections to the regularity of the organization, or to the jurisdiction of the judicatory, or to the sufficiency of the charges and specifications in form or in legal effect, or any other substantial objection affecting the order or regularity of the proceeding, on which objections the parties shall be heard." It is necessary, both in my own interest and in the interest of Presbyterian law and discipline, to avail myself of this right, to file objections to the sufficiency of the charges and specifications in " form " and " in legal effect "; and to make several "substantial objections affecting the order and regularity of the proceeding."

It is far from my purpose to raise objections of a merely technical kind or to stay the probation of charges which are approved as sufficient or specifications that are recognized as relevant by the Presbytery of New York, or to obstruct the course of procedure prescribed by the General Assembly. My desire from the beginning is expressed in the words of the General Assembly in the act of reversal, "that the case may be brought to issue and tried on the merits thereof as speedily as may be practicable"; but the order of the Book of Discipline requires that all these preliminary questions shall first be decided by the Presbytery, before I can plead "guilty" or "not guilty." No one can ask, with propriety, that I should waive this right of preliminary objection in order to consent to a trial on charges and specifications that are irrelevant; or to permit procedure which is irregular or disorderly and which can only complicate the trial and prevent a definite and just verdict. However much I may desire a trial on the merits of the case and a speedy settlement of issues which are necessarily of more moment to me than they can be to any one else, the Book of Discipline makes the duty of the defendant very plain.

The Presbytery should consider that I am not only the defendant in the case, but I am also, by the law of the Presbyterian Church, the counsel for the defendant, and I am held responsible for the management of the case in all matters of law as well as in all matters of doctrine. I could easily waive my right as defendant, but I cannot waive my duties as counsel. My choice would be, rather to be condemned while insisting upon a strict compliance with the law and constitution of the Church, than to be acquitted by a violation of the constitution. I shall not violate the constitution in order to secure acquittal, and I cannot consent to a violation of the constitution on the part of those who are seeking my condemnation. I am looking to the future, and not merely to the present. No one shall be able to say, if I can help it, that I allowed the prosecution, or the Presbytery to take illegal action, or to establish dangerous precedents, without resistance and protest. I cannot yield to the impatience of friends on the one side, or the crowding of enemies on the other side.

(I.) I object that the Amended Charges put in my hands, November 9th, 1892, were finally disposed of by the dismissal of the case against me on November 4th, 1891; and that the Presbytery could not legally cite me a second time to answer to charges which they had dismissed. Under the Old Book of Discipline, the supreme court of the Church decided that where a case arises without an individual prosecutor, there is but one original party in the case, namely, the defendant (O. S. 1859, p. 543). There was no individual prosecutor in the case against me which you dismissed on November 4th, 1891. The Presbytery dismissed the case, and, the sole original party under the Old Book of Discipline having acquiesced, the case reached its end. But according to the New Book of Discipline, the Presbyterian Church in the United States of America is an original party, and that original party was represented by the Presbytery. When therefore the Presbytery dismissed the case, and both original parties acquiesced, there could be no appeal. The supreme court of the Church has decided that members of a court trying a case are not parties in the case and may not appeal. (Digest, p. 592.) Therefore, any members of the court who may have acted as appellants, have acted so without right, and any action taken on their appeal, is null and void. If any member of the Presbytery felt aggrieved by the dismissal of the case, he had the right of complaint to the Synod of New York. This right of complaint was exercised, and a complaint was filed with the Synod against the action of the Presbytery in dismissing the case. But the complainants obtained leave from the Synod to withdraw their complaint. Therefore, there remains no further legal challenge to the action of the Presbytery in dismissing the case, and its action should be regarded as final. Therefore, the court has no legal right to bring against me Amended Charges, which Charges have already been finally disposed of.

(II.) I object to the order and regularity of the proceeding in the Presbytery, in any and every action taken against me since the dismissal of the said Charges on November 4th, 1891.

(1). I object that you allowed the floor to a committee to bring in Amended Charges, which committee claimed to be a committee of prosecution, an original party, and virtually and practically independent of the Presbytery; notwithstanding the fact that the minutes of the Presbytery show that no such committee was ever appointed by the Presbytery.

(2). I object that the right of the committee to act in any of these three capacities is challenged before the Synod of New York by a complaint signed by more than one-third of the Presbytery, and that such a complaint acts as a stay to all further proceeding until it has been determined by the Synod, and that therefore your action in proceeding to reopen the case against me with Amended Charges is illegal and disorderly.

(3). I object to the action of the Presbytery in sustaining the moderator in his decision that my objection to the status of the committee prior to the presentation of the Amended Charges was out of order, and in permitting the said committee to argue on behalf of their claim to be a prosecuting committee and an original party, and in refusing to allow me my legal right of argument against said claim.

Therefore I object to the entire procedure of the Presbytery in allowing the said committee to present Amended Charges; in serving these Charges upon me, and in citing me to appear and to answer to them, as altogether unconstitutional and illegal.

It may be said in reply to these objections that the General Assembly, by its action at Portland, reversed the action of the Presbytery of New York in the dismissal of the case, and remanded it to the Presbytery of New York for a new trial; and that therefore the Presbytery have no choice in the matter; they must submit to the action of the General Assembly and proceed with the case. But the Presbytery is not shut up to this procedure. It is the right of the Presbytery under the circumstances to send up a memorial to the next General Assembly, calling their attention to the fact that the Presbytery cannot proceed without a violation of the constitution of the Church; and asking them finally to determine all the preliminary constitutional questions before any further action shall be taken.

But it is not for me to advise the Presbytery what course they should pursue. I have done my duty in filing these objections. I have only this further word, that, if the Presbytery decide against me, I shall proceed under protest, and with the reservation of all legal rights of securing such redress in the higher courts as may seem necessary.

(III.) I object to the Amended Charges, that they do not comply with the law respecting amendment; and that they violate the express directions of the last General Assembly.

The law of amendment of charges is the following:

"The judicatory . . . . may permit, in the furtherance of justice, amendments to the specifications or

charges, not changing the general nature of the same "
(22).

The direction of the General Assembly was that the Presbytery should comply with this law, and " permit the prosecuting committee to amend the specifications or charges, not changing the general nature of the same, if, in the furtherance of justice, it be necessary to amend."

I object that the "general nature" of the original charges has been changed in these Amended Charges, and that it is not "in the furtherance of justice" that these prosecutors should be allowed to amend the Charges as they have done. A superficial comparison of the two sets of Charges is sufficient to show that there have been radical and thoroughgoing changes. But no one could imagine how radical and extensive these changes are without a careful analysis and synthesis of them. The defendant was ready for trial on the merits of the case on November 9th, but it has taken him the full time allowed him to revise his defence in the face of these new charges.

A. *The Changes in the Nature of the Evidence.*

I object that radical changes in the general nature of the evidence have been made in the Amended Charges. (1). There has been an entire overhauling of the evidences from Holy Scripture. In the original Charges there were 244 verses of Holy Scripture cited under the 8 specifications. One hundred and eighty of these, that is about three-fourths of them, have been thrown out, and 22 new ones have been introduced. The lines of evidence from Holy Scripture needed rectification. I cannot say that the revision has been too radical. It

rather lacks in thoroughness.   In my opinion the prosecution would have acted wisely if they had thrown out
all of these texts as irrelevant, and had given up the
case altogether.   I call the attention of the Presbytery
to these great changes that have been made in the evidence, in order to inquire whether it is in the interest of
justice that the prosecution should play so fast and loose
with Holy Scripture ; and that they should be allowed
to compel the defendant to change his defence to suit
so capricious a selection of texts, selected originally to
prove one thing, and now to prove a number of very
different things.

(2). There has been an important change in the evidences from the Westminster Standards, both by omis-
sions and insertions, which has compelled me to entirely
rearrange my lines of defence.   A considerable change
has been made in the use of the several sections and
clauses of chapter I.   Chapter XIV. has been thrown
out and chapter II. has been introduced, with new
answers to questions in the Catechism.   These changes
have been in the interest of certain phases of doctrine
which have been cast aside and of certain other doctrines which have been introduced into the Charges.

(3). There has also been a considerable amount of
change in citations from the Inaugural Address, which
has raised a number of new questions of doctrine.   Of
the 19 passages cited in the original Charges, 7 have
been omitted from the Amended Charges and 6 new
ones have been inserted, all which is associated with cor-
responding changes in the formulation of the Charges.
All these changes of evidence I am willing to overlook
and to waive, but it seems proper to call the attention
of the Presbytery to the fickleness of the prosecution
and to their apparent feeling of insecurity in the evi-

dence they proffer. I cannot, however, refrain from stating my indignation that this committee should be permitted to waste so much of my valuable time to no purpose.

(4). I object to the relevancy of all the proofs from Scripture, Confession, and Catechisms. Let me clearly set before you what kind of proof is necessary in order to convict me of heresy under Presbyterian law. It is necessary for this court, if you would make a just verdict in the fear of God, to put the charges and specifications in definite forms of major and minor premises. The major premise or charge must represent that certain teachings are irreconcilably opposed to some essential doctrine of the Westminster Standards and Holy Scripture. The minor premise or specification must set forth some statement in my Inaugural Address, interpreted in a sense to which I consent, which is in conflict with said doctrine.

Proof from Holy Scripture and the Westminster Confession must be presented under the charges in order to prove that the doctrines asserted in the charges as essential doctrines are really essential doctrines. Under the specifications the prosecution are shut up to proof from my Inaugural that I teach therein the erroneous doctrines specified. An examination of the charges and specifications shows that they do no such thing. The proofs from Scripture and from Confession are all under the specifications when they should be under the charges. I therefore challenge the relevancy of all the proofs offered by the prosecution from the Confession and from Holy Scripture. The attention of the Presbytery is called to this fault. It may be corrected by a simple transfer of these proofs from the specifications to the charges if the Presbytery so desire.

(5). There is one objection to the evidence offered by the prosecution which I cannot waive. I object to their offer of evidence by the wholesale. They offer: " the whole of the said Inaugural Address, both the first and second editions, and all the works of the said Rev. Charles A. Briggs, D.D., quoted therein, in so far as they bear upon this case, also the appendix to the second edition of said Address, and all the works of the said Rev. Charles A. Briggs, D.D., quoted therein, in so far as they bear upon this case ; the whole of the Holy Scriptures, and the whole of the Standards of the Presbyterian Church in the United States of America."

This offer of evidence is in violation of the Book of Discipline, which rules that :

" The charge shall set forth the alleged offence ; and the specifications shall set forth the facts relied upon to sustain the charge. Each specification shall declare, as far as possible, the time, place, and circumstances, and shall be accompanied with the names of the witnesses to be cited for their support." (15.)

The facts relied upon to sustain the charge, are facts relating to the Inaugural Address by the limitations imposed upon the prosecution, and these facts should be specified. The law is that the evidence shall be as specific as possible; the time, place, and circumstances of the offence, and the names of witnesses must be given. When the evidence is documentary the place in the document must be given, the citations must be made. It is unlawful to bring in evidence the whole of the Inaugural, and all of my writings referred to therein; the prosecution should state in their specifications all the evidence from the Inaugural they propose to offer, so that the defendant may have time to consider it and respond to it. It is unlawful to offer the whole of the Holy Scriptures; they are obliged to state what texts of Scripture they offer in evidence in order that I may test them. It is unlawful to offer in evidence the whole of the Westminster Standards. They are obliged to state in their charges what precise doctrines of the Standards my teachings oppose, and they should state what passages of the Standards they offer in proof of such opposition. The Presbytery should compel the prosecution to adhere to the evidence given under the specifications. I challenge their right to use any other evidence, and I shall resist it to the uttermost.

Let the Presbytery consider what the prosecution might do if you grant them the privilege of offering in proof the whole of the Inaugural, and all my writings referred to therein, and the whole of Holy Scripture and the Standards. I have shown you what extensive changes in evidence they have made in the Amended Charges. I have called your attention to the labor involved in the change of my defence to meet these charges. Is it in the interest of justice that they should be allowed to make what changes they please in their evidence, at any time they please, whether immediately before I make my defence, or afterwards, when I am precluded from further argument? Is it in the interest of justice that they should be allowed to change their lines of attack after long premeditation, and force me to change my lines of defence without any warning whatever and without any time for preparation on my part? Is it in the interest of justice that they should again throw away the greater part of their evidence in the Amended Charges as they threw it away from the original Charges, and virtually and practically make new Charges in their argument, without the consent of the Presbytery? Is the evidence presented in the Specifications a mere cloud of dust to hide the real evidence which they hold in reserve to spring upon us at such time as they choose? I cannot for a moment think that you will allow such injustice to be done. I object to this wholesale offer of proof.

Have you considered what will be required of you, if you consent to this proposal of the prosecution? It will be necessary for you to employ a reader to read to you all of the contents of the Standards of the Church, all of Holy Scripture, the entire Inaugural Address, and all of my writings referred to therein. You are required by law to have all the proposed evidence before you. We cannot consent that the prosecution should pick and choose out of all this material such passages as they may desire when they argue on behalf of their Charges. Therefore I request, in the interests of law and of justice, that the Amended Charges be amended by striking out this objectionable proposition, and the prosecution be restricted to the evidence offered under the specifications of the Amended Charges.

B. *The Change in the Nature of the Charges.*

I object to the Amended Charges that the nature of the original Charges has been changed. The original Charges called attention to several doctrines taught by me, which, as it was claimed, were in conflict with the Standards. The only doctrine of the Standards with which conflict was alleged, was the cardinal doctrine "that the Scriptures of the Old and New Testaments are the only infallible rule of faith and practice."

 The Amended Charges allege conflict with nine essential doctrines of the Westminster Standards, as follows:

(1) That Holy Scripture is most necessary.

(2) That Holy Scripture is the rule of faith and practice.

(3) That Holy Scripture is the word of God written.

(4) That Holy Scripture is immediately inspired.

(5) That God is true, omniscient, and unchangeable.

(6) That Holy Scripture evidences itself to be the word of God by the consent of all the parts.

(7) That the infallible rule of interpretation of Scripture is the Scripture itself.

(8) That the processes of redemption are limited to this world.

(9) That the souls of believers are at their death at once made perfect in holiness.

The Amended Charges, therefore, allege that my teachings conflict with nine different doctrines of the Westminster Standards. The original Charges allege conflict with only one cardinal doctrine, which is included as one of the nine. Therefore it is evident that the general nature of the original Charges is changed by the introduction of eight new charges. I might ask the Presbytery to follow the direction of the General Assembly and the law of the Book of Discipline, and so amend these Amended Charges as to cast out of them these eight new Charges. If you adhere strictly to law, you must do it. But so far as I am concerned, I shall waive this objection as regards six of these new charges, and make my stand against two of them.

(1). Let us consider the last Charge first. This introduces a new Charge, namely, that my teaching conflicts with the essential doctrine " that the souls of believers are at their death at once made perfect in holiness." Inasmuch as the original second Charge neglected to state what doctrine of the Standards it was with which the doctrine of Progressive Sanctification after Death came in conflict, and this Amended Charge may be regarded as such a statement, I waive my objection to it, and I consent to go to trial on the VIIIth of the present Charges.

(2). Charges I. and II. agree in alleging conflict with the essential doctrine of the Holy Scripture and of the Standards, that Holy Scripture is most necessary and the rule of faith and practice. The original charge was limited to conflict with the cardinal doctrine that Holy Scripture is the rule of faith and practice. If these two charges had limited themselves to that essential doctrine they would be in proper form for trial; but they insert an additional essential doctrine, namely, that the Holy Scripture is most necessary. This changes the nature of the Charge, and you cannot legally allow it. I could waive this objection, were it not for two reasons. (1) The combination of two essential doctrines in one charge is in violation of the law of the charge which requires that the charge should state but one offence. This charge states two offences, and is, therefore, insufficient in form and legal effect. (2) It is not in the interest of justice that a defendant should be exposed to conviction for conflict with two doctrines in one charge: for he might easily be convicted by a minority vote. If a minority should be convinced that my teaching is in conflict with the essential doctrine that " Holy Scripture is most necessary"; and another minority composed of different persons should be convinced that my teaching is in conflict with the essential doctrine that " Holy Scripture is the rule of faith and practice "; these two minorities might become a majority and vote me guilty if the vote should be taken upon the two charges together, when a majority of votes would acquit me if a vote were taken on each charge separately.

It is my right to insist that this new charge be stricken out.   At the same time I am entirely willing to be tried on this charge as a separate charge if the Presbytery so desire.   This you may accomplish either by breaking up Charges I. and II. into two charges each, or by ruling that a vote shall be taken on each of the two items in Charges I. and II. separately.   This you must do in accordance with the Book of Discipline: "A charge shall not allege more than one offence; several charges against the same person, however, with the specifications under each of them, may be presented to the judicatory at one and the same time, and may, in the discretion of the judicatory, be tried together.   But, when several charges are tried at the same time, a vote on each charge must be separately taken."   (16.)

(3). I have the same objection to Charge III.   Three offences are alleged in this charge, namely, that my teachings are in conflict with the essential doctrine (1) That Holy Scripture is the word of God written; (2) that Holy Scripture is immediately inspired; and (3) that Holy Scripture is the rule of faith and practice. Only the first of the three was in the original specification.   The third was in the original charge of which that specification was a part.   But the second is an entirely new charge, and on that account transcends the nature of the original charge.   I ask the Presbytery, therefore, either to obey the law of the charge and throw out the new charge, because it transcends the nature of the original charge; or else to make three charges out of this one charge, or else to rule that there shall be three different votes upon it, as the law requires when there are three different charges.

(4). Charges V. and VI. are open to more serious objection.   They agree in alleging that my doctrines conflict with two essential doctrines, namely, (1) that the Holy Scripture evidences itself to be the word of God by the consent of all the parts, and (2) that the infallible rule of interpretation is the Scripture itself; both of which are new charges and therefore transcend the nature of the original Charge, which was solely that these teachings conflict with the cardinal doctrine that Holy Scripture is the infallible rule of faith and practice. Therefore, in law, you should either remove these charges because they change the nature of the original Charge, or else reinsert in these Charges the essential doctrine mentioned in the original Charge. At the same time I am willing to waive this objection and to go to trial on these charges, provided each of them is made into a distinct charge, or else that a separate vote shall be taken on each charge, as the law requires when there are several charges.

I have called the attention of the Presbytery to the fact that Charges I., II., III., V., and VI. violate the law of the Charge and are in conflict with the order of the General Assembly, in that they change the nature of the original Charge by introducing several new doctrines of the Standards and of Holy Scripture, and also by combining two or three offences in the same charge. It is for you to determine this objection and to take the responsibility for any violation of law. The only thing that I insist upon, in the interest of justice, is, that every offence alleged against me shall be acted upon by a separate vote. Only in this way can you comply with the law, that a vote on each charge shall be separately taken. Only by this procedure can you reach a just verdict.

(5). Two charges remain to be considered, namely, IV. and VII. I object to them on two grounds. (1)

These are new charges which so change the general nature of the original Charges that they cannot legally be allowed; and (2) that it is not in the interests of ustice that such Charges as these should be approved by the Presbytery of New York.

They are new charges.

(a). Charge IV. alleges that I teach a doctrine "which is contrary to the essential doctrine of the Holy Scripture and of the Standards of the said Church, that God is true, omniscient and unchangeable." This is an entirely new charge. There was nothing in any of the original Charges or specifications which intimated either directly or indirectly that I taught any doctrine which conflicted with the essential doctrine of the Attributes of God. Specification 7 of the original Charge claimed that my doctrine of Predictive Prophecy was " contrary to the essential doctrine that Holy Scripture is the infallible rule of faith and practice." But consider the difference between that specification and this Charge. If the prosecution wish to persist in this Charge they should be required to go on and show what they originally proposed, that this doctrine conflicts with the Westminster doctrine of Holy Scripture ; they cannot legally ask me to defend my teaching against the new allegation, that it conflicts with the Westminster doctrine of the Attributes of God. Of the 32 texts from Holy Scripture used under the original specification, all but five have been thrown out, and three new ones have been introduced ; and instead of citations from the 1st chapter of the Confession, they give citations from the 2d chapter of the Confession in proof of their position, thus showing by their use of evidence that they have a new charge to sustain.

(b). Charge VII. is a new charge, new in the statement of the doctrine imputed to me, and new in the statement of the essential doctrine with which my teaching is alleged to conflict.

" The Presbyterian Church in the United States of America charges the Rev. Charles A. Briggs, D.D., being a minister of said Church, and a member of the Presbytery of New York, with teaching that the processes of redemption extend to the world to come in the case of many who die in sin; which is contrary to the essential doctrine of Holy Scripture and the Standards of the said Church, that the processes of redemption are limited to this world."

That this is an entirely new charge appears not only from the new statements in the Charge itself, but also from the evidence adduced. (a). The citations here given from the Inaugural, with the exception of four lines which are also given under Charge.VIII., were not given in the original Charge II. at all. (b). The proofs from Holy Scripture here given are six in number, only one of which, that relating to Dives and Lazarus, was used in the original Charge II. and thus could be used equally well under Charge VIII.

Thus in all respects this is a new charge. On this account you cannot recognize it as a lawful amendment. You should strike it out of the Amended Charges.

1. I have another objection to Charges IV. and VII. I claim that it is not in the interests of justice that you should approve them. They charge me with teaching doctrines which I have expressly disclaimed.

(a). In my response, November 4th, 1891, I said: " Specification 7 alleges that 'Dr. Briggs teaches that predictive prophecy has been reversed by history, and that much of it has not been, and never can be fulfilled.' This specification makes invalid inferences and statements. The specification makes two serious changes in the sentence of the Inaugural. (1). It omits altogether the qualifying clause, 'if we insist upon the fulfilment of the details of the predictive prophecy of the Old Testament,' and (2) it substitutes for 'many of these predictions,' the careful statement of the Inaugural Address, 'predictive prophecy,' a general and comprehensive term; and thus alleges that the Address teaches that 'predictive prophecy has been reversed by history.' This allegation is entirely without justification from anything taught in the Inaugural Address, or any other of my writings. I have ever taught that the predictive prophecy of the Old Testament has been fulfilled in history, or will yet be fulfilled in history. I have shown in my book, entitled 'Messianic Prophecy,' that 'the details of predictive prophecy' belong to the symbolical and typical form, and were never designed to be fulfilled. I have shown the historical development of the entire series of Messianic predictions of the Old Testament, and pointed them toward the fulfilment in Jesus Christ our Saviour; and have urged that either they have been fulfilled at His first advent, are being fulfilled in His reign over His Church, or will be fulfilled at His second advent." (Case, pp. 42–43.) Thus I exposed the misquotation and misrepresentation, and disclaimed the imputed teachings.

The Charge makes two slight amendments by substituting "many of the Old Testament predictions" for "predictive prophecy," and "the great body of Messianic prediction" for "much of it," softening the one statement in order to make the other still more offensive. The reiteration of this misquotation and misrepresentation in a slightly modified form in Charge IV., after I have so distinctly exposed it and disclaimed it, is an offence against Christian courtesy and an imputation upon my veracity which this Presbytery should not tolerate.   It is not in the interest of justice that the prosecution should be allowed so to amend the Charges.

(*b*). Charge VII. charges me " with teaching that the processes of redemption extend to the world to come in the case of many who die in sin."

The prosecution impute this doctrine to me, notwithstanding the disclaimer of such teaching which has been submitted to the Presbytery on two different occasions. (1). Dr. Geo. Alexander laid before the Presbytery on October 5th, 1891, without consultation with me, my answers to the following questions of the Directors of the Union Theological Seminary :   " Do you hold what is commonly known as the doctrine of a future probation?   Do you believe in Purgatory?   Answer, No. Do you believe that the issues of this life are final, and that a man who dies impenitent will have no further opportunity of salvation?   Answer, Yes."

(2). In my response of Nov. 4th, 1891, I said : " If I had been charged with teaching second probation, or any probation whatever after death, I might have pointed to several of my writings in which this doctrine is distinctly disclaimed.   If the doctrine of purgatory had been imputed, or regeneration after death, or transition after death from the state of the condemned to the state of the justified, any and all of these could be disproved by my writings."   I ask the Presbytery in view of these disclaimers, if it is just, if it is honorable, if it is in accordance with Christian courtesy and gentlemanly propriety, for the prosecution to make such charges against me?

They put you in a dilemma.   Either you must with them challenge my veracity, or else you must permit them to present proof that my explanations of my teachings are erroneous, and that their explanations must be accepted as true. If you wish to challenge my veracity, you should do it under a moral charge, you cannot do it under a doctrinal charge. If you permit them to make such explanations and recognize them as valid you will engage in illegal procedure, for according to the decision of the supreme court of the Church in the Craighead case, "No man can rightly be convicted of heresy by inference or implication." "It is not right to charge any man with an opinion which he disavows."

For these reasons I object to Charges IV. and VII., and I demand óf the Presbytery that they comply with the law of the Church and reject them from the list of charges.

IV. There are other preliminary objections which I might make. But I refrain in order to save valuable time and to concentrate your attention upon such changes in the Amended Charges as the Presbytery ought itself to make in the interests of law and justice.

(1). The Prosecution have had sufficient opportunity to construct their Charges and to amend them. It is not in the interest of justice that they should have any further opportunity. They should be required to risk their charges in the form in which the Presbytery may now amend them.

(2). It is not in the interest of justice that I should be required to prepare a defence against another set of Charges. This is the third time that I have appeared before the Presbytery with a long and carefully prepared defence. Life is too short and the duties of life are too pressing to justify me in constantly readjusting my work to suit the intellectual and rhetorical processes of such unstable prosecutors. I have prepared my defence. I shall present it to the Presbytery if you will have it ; if not, I shall publish it to the world.

(3). It is not in the interest of justice that this Presbytery composed of more than an hundred ministers and half an hundred elders, whose time and strength are of inestimable value to their families, to their business associates, to society, to institutions of learning and of benevolence, and to the Church of God, should be wearied with this trial any longer than is absolutely necessary. Let the Presbytery amend the Charges in the interest of justice and in accordance with the law of the Church, and let us proceed to trial and determine so soon as possible the great issues which are involved to ourselves and to the Presbyterian Church.

The Presbytery are respectfully requested to pass upon these preliminary objections, in accordance with the Book of Discipline, which says: "The judicatory upon the filing of such objections shall, or on its motion may, determine all such preliminary objections."

C. A. BRIGGS.

November 28th, 1892.

IV.

THE ACTION OF THE PRESBYTERY OF NEW YORK ON THESE PRELIMINARY OBJECTIONS; AND THE COMPLAINTS OF PROFESSOR BRIGGS TO THE SYNOD OF NEW YORK.

A.

The Presbytery by a vote of 70 to 49 instructed the Committee to strike out Charge IV.

B.

The Presbytery by a vote of 74 to 54 instructed the Committee to strike out Charge VII.

C.

The Presbytery by a large majority declined to sustain the following Objection:

"*I object that the Charges put in my hand November 9th, 1892, were fully disposed of by the dismissal of the case against me on November 4th, 1891, and that the Presbytery could not legally cite me a second time to answer to charges which they had dismissed.*"

Against this action of the Presbytery, Prof. Briggs entered the following complaint to the Synod of New York:

Complaint is hereby made before the Synod of New York by the persons whose names are appended below, being persons subject and submitting to the jurisdiction of the Presbytery of New York, in accordance with Sections 83 and 86 of the Revised Book of Discipline, against the action of the Presbytery of New York, November 29, 1892, in refusing to sustain the *first objection* made by the defendant to the Amended Charges in the case of the Rev. Chas. A. Briggs, D.D., viz.:

"(I.) I object that the charges put in my hands November 9th, 1892, were finally disposed of by the dismissal of the case against me on November 4th, 1891, and that the Presbytery could not legally cite me a second time to answer to charges which they had dismissed."

Against this refusal of the Presbytery, complaint is made for the following reasons:

1. When the Presbytery dismissed the case, both the original parties acquiesced, viz., the Presbyterian Church in the United States of America, represented by the Presbytery, on the one side, and the defendant on the other. Therefore there could be no legal appeal, and no legal reopening of the case, since an appeal can be taken only by one of the original parties.

2. The Supreme Court of the Church has decided [Moore's Digest, 1873, p. 592, 1886, p. 692], that members of a court trying a case are not parties in the case, and may not appeal. Therefore, any members of the court who may have acted as appellants, have so acted without right, and any action taken on their appeal is null and void.

3. A complaint was filed with the Synod of New York against the action of the Presbytery in dismissing the case, but the complainants obtained leave from the Synod to withdraw their complaint. Therefore there remained no legal challenge to the action of the Presbytery in dismissing the case, and this action should have been regarded as final.

4. The Presbytery had no legal right to bring against the defendant Amended Charges, when the original charges had already been finally disposed of.

For these reasons, notice of complaint having been duly given within ten days after the action complained of, according to Section 84 of the Revised Book of Discipline, complaint is hereby made in due form to the next higher judicatory, being the Synod of New York, against the action of the Presbytery of New York above described, and the Synod is most respectfully and earnestly requested to entertain this complaint and to take therein such action as shall in its judgment appear wise and likely to promote good order, justice, and the peace, purity, and welfare of the Church of Christ.

[Signed],   C. A. BRIGGS,
                             FRANCIS BROWN,
                                  etc., etc.

D.

The Presbytery by a large majority declined to sustain the following Objection and the points enumerated in it:

"*I object to the order and regularity of the proceeding in the Presbytery, in any and every action taken against me since the dismissal of the said charges on November 4th, 1891.*"

Against this action of the Presbytery Prof. Briggs entered the following complaint to the Synod of New York:

Complaint is hereby made before the Synod of New York by the persons whose names are appended below, being persons subject and submitting to the jurisdiction of the Presbytery of New York, in accordance with Sections 83 and 86 of the Revised Book of Discipline, against the action of the Presbytery of New York, November 29, 1892, in refusing to sustain the *second objection* made by the defendant to the Amended Charges in the case of the Rev. Charles A. Briggs, D.D., viz.:

"(II.) I object to the order and regularity of the proceeding in the Presbytery, in any and every action taken against me since the dismissal of the said Charges on November 4th, 1891."

Against this refusal of the Presbytery complaint is made for the following reasons:

1. The proceeding in the Presbytery was illegal in that the floor was allowed to a Committee to bring in Amended Charges, which Committee claimed to be a Committee of Prosecution, an original party, and virtually and practically independent of the Presbytery, notwithstanding the fact that the minutes of the Presbytery show that no such Committee was ever appointed by the Presbytery.

2. The proceeding in the Presbytery was illegal in that the Presbytery reopened the case with Amended Charges, while the right of the Committee aforesaid to act as a Committee of Prosecution was challenged before the Synod of New York by a complaint signed by more than one-third of the Presbytery; this complaint being, at the time of the action now complained of, not yet determined by the Synod.

3. The proceeding in the Presbytery was illegal in that the Presbytery sustained the Moderator, November 9th, 1892, in his decision that an objection offered to the status of the Committee was at that time out of order, permitting the said Committee to argue on behalf of their claim to be a Prosecuting Committee and an original party, and refusing to allow to the defendant his legal right of argument in support of his objection against said claim.

4. Therefore the entire procedure of the Presbytery in allowing the said Committee to present Amended Charges, in serving these Charges upon the defendant, and in citing him to appear and answer to them, was altogether unconstitutional and illegal.

For these reasons, notice of complaint having been duly given less than ten days after the action complained of, according to Section 84 of the Revised Book of Discipline, complaint is hereby made in due form to the next higher judicatory, being the Synod of New York, against the action of the Presbytery of New York above described, and the Synod is most respectfully and earnestly requested to entertain this complaint, and to take therein such action as shall in its judgment appear wise and likely to promote good order, justice, and the peace, purity, and welfare of the Church of Christ.

[Signed], C. A. BRIGGS,
FRANCIS BROWN,
etc., etc.

E.

The Presbytery by a vote of 71 to 56 took the following action:

"Without sustaining the general objection to the relevancy of the Scripture and Confessional Proofs, this Presbytery would direct that they be transferred from the specifications to the charges."

F.

The Presbytery by a vote of 70 to 68 declined to strike out from the Amended Charges and Specifications the following proffer of wholesale evidence:

"The Presbyterian Church in the United States of America, represented by the undersigned Prosecuting

Committee, offers in evidence the whole of the said Inaugural Address, both the first and second editions, and
all the works of the said Rev. Charles A. Briggs, D.D.,
quoted therein, in so far as they bear upon this case;
also the appendix to the second edition of said Address,
and all the works of the said Rev. Charles A. Briggs,
D.D., quoted therein, in so far as they bear upon this
case; the whole of the Holy Scriptures and the whole
of the Standards of the Presbyterian Church in the
United States of America."

Against this action of the Presbytery Prof. Briggs entered the following complaint to the Synod of New York:

Complaint is hereby made before the Synod of New
York by the persons whose names are appended below,
being persons subject and submitting to the jurisdiction
of the Presbytery of New York, in accordance with Sections 83 and 86 of the Revised Book of Discipline,
against the action of the Presbytery of New York,
November 30th, 1892, in refusing by a vote of 70 to 68,
to strike out from the Amended Charges in the case of
the Rev. Charles A. Briggs, D.D., the concluding paragraph, as follows:

"The Presbyterian Church in the United States of
America, represented by the undersigned Prosecuting
Committee, offers in evidence the whole of the said
Inaugural Address, both the first and second editions,
and all the works of the said Rev. Charles A. Briggs,
D.D., quoted therein, in so far as they bear upon this
case; also the appendix to the second edition of said
Address, and all the works of the said Rev. Charles A.
Briggs, D.D., quoted therein, in so far as they bear upon
this case; the whole of the Holy Scriptures and the
whole of the Standards of the Presbyterian Church in
the United States of America."

Against the refusal of the Presbytery to strike out this paragraph, complaint is made for the following reasons:

1. The offer of evidence made in this paragraph was in violation of Section 15 of the Revised Book of Discipline, which requires that "the charge shall set forth the alleged offence; and the specifications shall set forth the facts relied upon to sustain the charge. Each specification shall declare, as far as possible, the time, place, and circumstances, and shall be accompanied with the names of the witnesses to be cited for its support."

2. When the evidence is documentary, the place in the document must be given, and the citations must be made, in order that the defendant may have time to consider and respond to every part of the evidence.

3. It was not in the interest of justice that the prosecution should be permitted to offer evidence in this wholesale manner, and hence this paragraph in the Amended Charges was illegal, since only amendments "in the furtherance of justice" are permitted by the Book of Discipline [Section 22].

For these reasons notice of complaint having been duly given, less than ten days after the action complained of, according to Section 84 of the Revised Book of Discipline, complaint is hereby made in due form to the next higher judicatory, being the Synod of New York, against the action of the Presbytery of New York above described, and the Synod is most respectfully and earnestly requested to entertain this complaint and to take therein such action as shall in its judgment appear wise and likely to promote good order, justice, and the peace, purity, and welfare of the Church of Christ.

[Signed],   C. A. BRIGGS,
                 FRANCIS BROWN,
                      etc., etc.

G.

The Presbytery resolved by a large majority that "in view of the conditional waiver made by the defendant, the Presbytery, without passing upon his objections to Charges 1, 2, 3, 5, and 6, rules that in taking the vote each of the items in these charges as indicated by numerals in the objections filed shall be voted upon separately."

H.

The prosecution offered in evidence "the whole of the said Inaugural Address, both the first and second editions" . . . . "the works of the Rev. Charles A. Briggs, D.D., quoted therein, in so far as they bear upon this case" . . . . "the Appendix to the second edition of said Address and all the works of the said Rev. Charles A. Briggs, D.D., quoted therein, in so far as they bear upon this case" . . . . "the whole of the Holy Scriptures and the whole of the Standards of the Presbyterian Church in the United States of America."

Prof. Briggs called "for the reading of this proposed evidence so far as it bears upon this case." The Presbytery, instead of requiring the prosecution to read the proposed documentary evidence, decided by a majority vote:

"That the evidence offered by the prosecution be considered by us competent."

Against this action of the Presbytery, Prof. Briggs entered the following complaint to the Synod of New York:

Complaint is hereby made before the Synod of New York by the persons whose names are appended below, being persons subject and submitting to the jurisdiction of the Presbytery of New York, in accordance with Sections 83 and 86 of the Revised Book of Discipline against the action of the Presbytery of New York, December 1, 1892, in voting " that the evidence offered by the prosecution be considered competent."

Against this action complaint is made for the following reasons:

1. The evidence referred to in this action was not before the Presbytery, because it was not read in the hearing of the Presbytery.

2. The defendant called for the reading of the proposed evidence so far as it bears upon the case [Stenographic Report, p. 360] in order that he might have all the evidence before him; but this, his just and reasonable request, was refused by the Presbytery in the above action.

3. By the action complained of the Presbytery resolved to proceed to the adjudication of a case in which a large part of the evidence offered by the prosecution was neither read to the court, nor in any other specific and detailed manner brought to the knowledge of the court and the defendant.

For these reasons notice of complaint having been duly given, less than ten days after the action complained of, according to Section 84 of the Revised Book of Discipline, complaint is hereby made in due form to the next higher judicatory, being the Synod of New York, against the action of the Presbytery of New York above described, and the Synod is most respectfully and earnestly requested to entertain this complaint, and to take therein such action as shall in its judgment appear wise and likely to promote good order, justice, and the peace, purity, and welfare of the Church of Christ.

[Signed],   C. A. BRIGGS,
FRANCIS BROWN,
etc., etc.

V.

THE EVIDENCE SUBMITTED TO THE PRESBYTERY OF NEW YORK BY PROFESSOR BRIGGS, DECEMBER 5, 1892.

Mr. Moderator, Ministers and Elders of the Presbytery of New York:

Inasmuch as my preliminary objection to the presentation by the prosecution of evidence by the wholesale, and my request for the reading of their evidence, have been overruled by the Presbytery, I submit to your decisions with the reservation of all rights of appeal and complaint, and claim the same privilege for the defendant which you have granted to the prosecution.

I submit the following documentary evidence "in so far as it bears upon this case," reading such portions as I desire to bring before you at this time, and reserving the right to read such other portions as I may desire to use in the several stages of the defence.

(1). I offer in evidence the whole of the Holy Scriptures of the Old and New Testaments in the following texts and versions: (*a*). The Hebrew text of the Old Testament, Theile's edition. (*b*). The Septuagint version of the Old Testament, Sweete's edition. (*c*). The Greek text of the New Testament, edition of Westcott and Hort. (*d*). The Revised English Version of the Old and New Testaments. (*e*). The Authorized Version, the Variorum Reference edition.

I submit these without reading, according to the ruling of the Presbytery.

(2). I offer in evidence the Standards of the Presbyterian Church in the United States of America, in the amended edition published by the Presbyterian Board of Publication, 1891. I submit these without reading according to the ruling of the Presbytery, with the exception of a few passages which I shall now read:

CHAP. I., 5, 6, 7, *The Westminster Confession.*

"5. We may be moved and induced by the testimony of the church to an high and reverent esteem for the Holy Scripture; and the heavenliness of the matter, the efficacy of the doctrine, the majesty of the style, the consent of all the parts, the scope of the whole, (which is to give all glory to God), the full discovery it makes of the only way of man's salvation, the many other incomparable excellencies, and the entire perfection thereof, are arguments whereby it doth abundantly evidence itself to be the word of God; yet, notwithstanding, our full persuasion and assurance of the infallible truth, and divine authority thereof, is from the inward work of the Holy Spirit, bearing witness by and with the word in our hearts.

"6. The whole counsel of God, concerning all things necessary for his own glory, man's salvation, faith, and life, is either expressly laid down in Scripture, or by good and necessary consequence may be deduced from Scripture: unto which nothing at any time is to be added, whether by new revelations of the Spirit, or traditions of men. Nevertheless we acknowledge the inward illumination of the Spirit of God to be necessary for the saving understanding of such things as are revealed in the word; and that there are some circumstances concerning the worship of God, and the government of the church, common to human actions and societies, which are to be ordered by the light of nature and Christian prudence, according to the general rules of the word, which are always to be observed.

"7. All things in Scripture are not alike plain in themselves, nor alike clear unto all; yet those things which are necessary to be known, believed, and observed, for salvation, are so clearly propounded and opened in some places of Scripture or other, that not only the learned, but the unlearned, in a due use of the ordinary means, may attain unto a sufficient understanding of them."

CHAP. X., 1: *of Effectual Calling.*

" All those whom God hath predestinated unto life, and those only, he is pleased, in his appointed and accepted time, effectually to call, by his word and Spirit, out of that state of sin and death, in which they are by nature, to grace and salvation by Jesus Christ; enlightening their minds spiritually and savingly, to understand the things of God; taking away their heart of stone, and giving unto them an heart of flesh; renewing their will, and by his almighty power determining them to that which is good, and effectually drawing them to Jesus Christ, yet so as they come most freely, being made willing by his grace."

CHAP. XIII., 1, 2, 3: *of Sanctification.*

" They who are effectually called and regenerated, having a new heart and a new spirit created in them, are further sanctified, really and personally, through the virtue of Christ's death and resurrection, by his word and Spirit dwelling in them: the dominion of the whole body of sin is destroyed, and the several lusts thereof are more and more weakened and mortified; and they more and more quickened and strengthened, in all saving graces, to the practice of true holiness, without which no man shall see the Lord."

" 2. This sanctification is throughout in the whole man, yet imperfect in this life: there abideth still some remnants of corruption in every part, whence ariseth a continual and irreconcilable war, the flesh lusting against the Spirit, and the Spirit against the flesh.

" 3. In which war, although the remaining corruption for a time may much prevail, yet, through the continual supply of strength from the sanctifying Spirit of Christ, the regenerate part doth overcome: and so the saints grow in grace, perfecting holiness in the fear of God."

CHAP. XVIII., 1, 2: *of the Assurance of Grace and Salvation.*

" Although hypocrites, and other unregenerate men, may vainly deceive themselves with false hopes and carnal presumptions of being in the favor of God and estate of salvation; which hope of theirs shall perish: yet such as truly believe in the Lord Jesus, and love him in sincerity, endeavoring to walk in all good conscience before him, may in this life be certainly assured that they are in a state of grace, and may rejoice in the hope of the glory of God; which hope shall never make them ashamed.

"2. This certainty is not a bare conjectural and probable persuasion, grounded upon a fallible hope; but an infallible assurance of faith, founded upon the divine truth of the promises of salvation, the inward evidence of those graces unto which these promises are made, the testimony of the Spirit of adoption witnessing with our spirits that we are the children of God: which Spirit is the earnest of our inheritance, whereby we are sealed to the day of redemption."

CHAP. XX., 2 : *of Christian Liberty, and Liberty of Conscience.*

"2. God alone is Lord of the conscience, and hath left it free from the doctrines and commandments of men which are in anything contrary to his word, or beside it, in matters of faith or worship. So that to believe such doctrines, or to obey such commandments out of conscience, is to betray true liberty of conscience; and the requiring an implicit faith, and an absolute and blind obedience, is to destroy liberty of conscience, and reason also."

CHAP. XXV., 3 : *of the Church.*

"3. Unto this catholic visible church, Christ hath given the ministry, oracles, and ordinances of God, for the gathering and perfecting of the saints, in this life, to the end of the world: and doth by his own presence and Spirit, according to his promise, make them effectual thereunto."

CHAP. XXVII., 3 : *of the Sacraments.*

"3. The grace which is exhibited in or by the sacraments, rightly used, is not conferred by any power in them, neither doth the efficacy of a sacrament depend upon the piety or intention of him that doth administer it, but upon the work of the Spirit, and the word of institution, which contains, together with a precept authorizing the use thereof, a promise of benefit to worthy receivers."

LARGER CATECHISM, QUEST. 90 :   "*What shall be done to the righteous at the day of judgment ?*"

"A.   At the day of judgment, the righteous, being caught up to Christ in the clouds, shall be set on his right hand, and there openly acknowledged and acquitted, shall join with him in the judging of reprobate angels and men : and shall be received into heaven, where they shall be fully and forever freed from all sin and misery; filled with inconceivable joys; made perfectly holy and happy both in body and soul, in the company of innumerable saints and angels, but especially in the immediate vision and fruition of God the Father, of our Lord Jesus Christ, and of the Holy Spirit, to all eternity.   And this is the perfect and full communion, which the members of the invisible church shall enjoy with Christ in glory, at the resurrection and day of judgment."

SHORTER CATECHISM, QUEST. 2 :   "*What rule hath God given to direct us how we may glorify and enjoy him ?*"

"A.   The word of God, which is contained in the Scriptures of the Old and New Testaments, is the only rule to direct us how we may glorify and enjoy him."

BOOK OF DISCIPLINE, *Sect.* 1.

"I.   Discipline is the exercise of that authority, and the application of that system of laws, which the Lord Jesus Christ has appointed in his church."

(3).   I shall offer in evidence the Inaugural Address as published in the first edition with accompanying documents under the title, "The Edward Robinson Chair of Biblical Theology," as published in the second edition with an appendix, and as published in a third and fourth editions with appendixes all under the title, "*The Authority of Holy Scripture.*"   I beg leave to put a third edition of these documents in the hands of every member of the court in place of reading them, except so far as the following extracts which I shall now read in order to put the citations made by the prosecution in the light of their context.   I shall read pp. 4–6:

' "Biblical Theology is, at the present time, the vantage ground for the solution of those important problems in religion, doctrine, and morals that are compelling the attention of the men of our times. The Bible is the Word of God, and its authority is divine authority that determines the faith and life of men. Biblical scholars have been long held in bondage to ecclesiasticism and dogmatism. But modern Biblical criticism has won the battle of freedom. The accumulations of long periods of traditional speculation and dogmatism have been in large measure removed, and the Bible itself stands before the men of our time in a commanding position, such as it never has enjoyed before. On all sides it is asked, not what do the creeds teach, what do the theologians say, what is the authority of the Church, but what does the Bible itself teach us? It is the office of Biblical Theology to answer this question. It is the culmination of the Work of Exegesis. It rises on a complete induction through all the departments of Biblical study to a comprehensive grasp of the Bible as a whole, in the unity and variety of the sum of its teaching. It draws the line with the teaching of the Bible. It fences off from the Scriptures all the speculations, all the dogmatic elaborations, all the doctrinal adaptations that have been made in the history of doctrine in the Church. It does not deny their propriety and importance, but it insists upon the three-fold distinction as necessary to truth and theological honesty, that the theology of the Bible is one thing, the only infallible authority; the theology of the creeds is another thing, having simply ecclesiastical authority ; and the theology of the theologians, or Dogmatic Theology, is a third thing, which has no more authority than any other system of human construction. It is well known that until quite recent times, and even at present in some quarters, the creeds have lorded it over the Scriptures, and the dogmaticians have lorded it over the creeds, so that in its last analysis the authority in the Church has been, too often, the authority of certain theologians. Now, Biblical Theology aims to limit itself strictly to the theology of the Bible itself. Biblical theologians are fallible men, and doubtless it is true, that they err in their interpretation of the Scriptures, as have others ; but it is the aim of the discipline to give the theology of the Bible pure and simple; and the inductive and historical methods that determine the working of the department are certainly favorable to an objective presentation of the subject and are unfavorable to the intrusion of subjective fancies and circumstantial considerations. It will be my aim, so long as I remain in the chair, to accomplish this ideal as far as possible. Without fear or favor I shall teach the truth of God's word as I find it. The theology of the Bible is much simpler, richer, and grander than any of the creeds or dogmatic systems. These have been built upon select portions of the Bible, and there is capriciousness of selection in them all. But Biblical Theology makes no selection of texts—it uses the entire Bible in all its passages, and in every single passage, giving each its place and importance in the unfolding of divine revelation. To Biblical Theology the Bible is a mine of untold wealth ; treasures, new and old, are in its storehouses ; all its avenues lead in one way or another, to the presence of the living God and the divine Saviour."

Page 10: "President Butler addressed Professor Briggs as follows:

" On behalf of the Board of Directors, and in accordance with the constitution of the 'Union Theological Seminary in the City of New York,' I call upon you to '*make and subscribe*' the '*declaration*' required of each member of the Faculty of this institution."

"Thereupon Professor Briggs made the 'declaration' as follows :

" 'I believe the Scriptures of the Old and New Testaments to be the Word of God, the only infallible rule of faith and practice ; and I do now, in the presence of God and the Directors of this Seminary, solemnly and sincerely receive and adopt the Westminster Confession of Faith, as containing the system of doctrine taught in the Holy Scriptures. I do also, in like manner, approve of the Presbyterian Form of Government ; and I do solemnly promise that I will not teach or inculcate anything which shall appear to me to be subversive of the said system of doctrines, or of the principles of said Form of Government, so long as I shall continue to be a Professor in the Seminary.' "

I ask the court to read especially pages 23–29 ; 32–36 ; 52–55. I read from the appendixes, page 85 :

"When it was said, 'There are historically three great fountains of divine authority—the Bible, the Church, and the Reason '—I did not say, and I did not give any one the right to infer from anything whatever in the Inaugural Address or in any of my writings, that I co-ordinated the Bible, the Church, and the Reason."

I ask the court to read pages 85-89; and I read also the following, on page 111 :

"The views that I have expressed with regard to sanctification after death should be carefully distinguished from the Roman Catholic doctrine of Purgatory on the one side and the Arminian doctrine of Probation on the other side. Both of these I reject. I build on the Biblical doctrine of the Middle State and the invariable statement of the New Testament that the second advent of Jesus Christ is the goal of sanctification. Rom. viii. 29-30; 1 Cor. i. 8; Eph. iv. 13-26; Phil. i. 6; 1 Thess. iii. 13; v. 23; 2 Peter iii. 13-14; John iii. 2-3. There is not a passage in the Bible that teaches either directly or indirectly immediate sanctification at death."

(4). I offer in evidence the following official documents in so far as they bear upon this case.

(a). The Confession of Faith, together with the Larger and Lesser Catechisms composed by the reverend assembly of divines sitting at Westminster, edition of 1658.

(b). The Minutes of the Sessions of the Westminster Assembly, Nov., 1644, to March, 1649, edited for the committee of the Church of Scotland, with an introduction by Alex. F. Mitchell, Edinburgh, 1874.

(c). The Records of the Presbyterian Church in the United States of America, published by the Presbyterian Board of Publication.

(d). The Minutes of the Presbyterian Church in the United States of America, 1789-1892.

(f). The Minutes of the Presbytery of New York.

(g). The Stenographical Report of the meeting of Presbytery, October 5th, 1891.

(*h*). The Stenographical Report of the meeting of Presbytery, November 4th, 1891.

(*i*). The Stenographical Report of the sessions of the General Assembly at Portland, May 26–30, 1892.

(*j*). The Creeds of Christendom, by Dr. Schaff.

I submit these documents without reading in accordance with the ruling of the Presbytery, with the exception of the following extract which I shall read to the court at this time, from the minutes of Presbytery, Oct. 5th, 1891 :

"WHEREAS, the Presbytery of New York, at its meeting in May last, on account of utterances contained in an inaugural address, delivered January 20, 1891, appointed a committee to formulate charges against the author of that address, Rev. Charles A. Briggs, D.D., and, whereas, since that action was taken, the accused has supplemented those utterances by responding to certain categorical questions.

" Question I. Do you consider the Bible, the Church, and the Reason as co-ordinate sources of authority ?
Answer. No.

" Or, do you believe the Scriptures of the Old and New Testaments to be the only infallible rule of faith and practice ?
Answer. Yes.

" Question II. When you use the word 'reason,' do you include the conscience and the religious feeling ?
Answer. Yes.

" Question III. Would you accept the following as a satisfactory definition of Inspiration : Inspiration is such a divine direction as to secure an infallible record of God's revelation in respect to both fact and doctrine ?
Answer. Yes.

" Question IV. Do you believe the Bible to be inerrant in all matters concerning faith and practice and in everything in which it is a revelation from God, or a vehicle of Divine truth, and that there are no errors that disturb its infallibility in these matters, or in its records of the historic events and institutions with which they are inseparably connected ?
Answer. Yes.

"Question V. Do you believe that the miracles recorded in Scripture are due to an extraordinary exercise of divine energy, either directly or mediately through holy men?

Answer. Yes.

"Question VI. Do you hold what is commonly known as the doctrine of a future probation? Do you believe in purgatory?

Answer. No.

"Question VII. Do you believe that the issues of this life are final, and that a man who dies impenitent will have no further opportunity of salvation?

Answer. Yes.

"Question VIII. Is your theory of progressive sanctification such that it will permit you to say that you believe that when a man dies in the faith, he enters the middle state regenerated, justified and sinless?

Answer. Yes.

(Signed),   C. A. BRIGGS.

I hereby certify that the foregoing is a true copy from the Minutes of the Board of Directors of Union Theological Seminary of the City of New York.

E. M. KINGSLEY,

NEW YORK, Oct. 5, 1891.   Recorder."

(5). Inasmuch as the prosecution have put in evidence all the works of Dr. Briggs quoted in the first and second editions of the Inaugural Address "so far as they bear upon this case," the defendant puts in evidence all the works of Dr. Briggs "in so far as they bear upon this case." These are put in evidence without reading in accordance with the ruling of the Presbytery, save the following testimony which I shall read at the present time.

(a). Address on occasion of his inauguration as Davenport professor of Hebrew and the Cognate languages in the Union Theological Seminary, October, 1876. I read from pages 6-7:

"The history of the Church, and Christian experience, have shown that in so far as the other branches of theology have separated themselves from this fundamental discipline, and in proportion to the neglect of Exegetical Theology, the Church has fallen into a dead orthodoxy of scholasticism, has lost its hold upon the masses of mankind, so that with its foundations undermined, it has yielded but feeble resistance to the onsets of infidelity. And it has ever been that the reformation or revival has come through the resort to the sacred oracles, and the organization of a freshly-stated body of doctrine, and fresh methods of evangelization derived therefrom. We thus have reason to thank God that heresy and unbelief so often drive us to our citadel, the sacred Scriptures, and force us back to the impregnable fortress of divine truth, in order that, depending no longer merely upon human weapons and defences, we may use rather the divine, and thus reconquer all that may have been lost, and advance a stage onward in our victorious progress toward the end. Our adversaries may overthrow our systems of theology, our confessions and catechisms, our church organizations and methods of work, for these are, after all, human productions, the hastily thrown up out-works of the truth; but they can never contend successfully against the Word of God that liveth and abideth forever (1 Peter i. 23), which, though the heavens fall and the earth pass away, will not fail in one jot or tittle from the most complete fulfilment (Matt. v. 18), which will shine in new beauty and glory as its parts are one by one searchingly examined, and · which will prove itself not only invincible, but all-conquering, as point after point is most hotly contested, until at last it claims universal obedience as the pure and faultless mirror of Him who is Himself the brightness of the Father's glory and the express image of His person. (2 Cor. iii. 18; Heb. i. 3).

Also from pages 15–16:

" Whatever may have been the prevailing views in the church with reference to the Pentateuch, Psalter, or any other book of Scripture, they will not deter the conscientious exegete an instant from accepting and teaching the results of a historical and critical study of the writings themselves. It is just here that Christian theologians have greatly injured the cause of the truth and the Bible by dogmatizing in a department where it is least of all appropriate, and, indeed, to the highest degree improper, as if our faith depended at all upon these human opinions re-

specting the Word of God; as if the Scriptures could be bene-
fited by defending the indefensible, whereas by these frequent
and shameful defeats and routs these traditionalists bring dis-
grace and alarm even into the impregnable fortress itself and
prejudice the sincere inquirer against the Scriptures, as if these
were questions of orthodoxy or piety, or of allegiance to the
Word of God or the symbols of the church. Our standards
teach that 'the Word of God is the only rule of faith and obedience,' and that 'the authority of the Holy Scripture, for which
it ought to be believed and obeyed, dependeth not upon the
testimony of any man or church, but wholly upon God, the
author thereof.' How unorthodox it is, therefore, to set up another rule of prevalent opinion as a stumbling-block to those
who would accept the authority of the Word of God alone. So
long as the Word of God is honored, and its decisions regarded
as final, what matters it if a certain book be detached from the
name of one holy man and ascribed to another, or classed among
those with unknown authors? Are the laws of the Pentateuch
any less divine, if it should be proved that they are the product
of the experience of God's people from Moses to Josiah? Is
the Psalter to be esteemed any the less precious that the Psalms
should be regarded as the product of many poets singing
through many centuries the sacred melodies of God-fearing souls,
responding from their hearts, as from a thousand-stringed lyre,
to the touch of the Holy One of Israel? Is the book of Job
less majestic and sublime, as, the noblest monument of sacred
poetry, it stands before us in its solitariness, with unknown author, unknown birth-place, and from an unknown period of history? Are the ethical teachings of the Proverbs, the Song of
Songs, and Ecclesiastes, any the less solemn and weighty, that
they may not be the product of Solomon's wisdom alone, but of
the reflection of many holy wise men of different epochs, gathered
about Solomon as their head? Is the epistle to the Hebrews
any less valuable for its clear presentation of the fulfilment of
the Old Testament priesthood and sacrifice in the work of
Christ, that it must be detached from the name of Paul? Let
us not be so presumptuous, so irreverent to the Word of God, so
unbelieving with reference to its inherent power of convincing
and assuring the seekers for the truth, as to condemn any sin-

cere and candid inquirer as a heretic or a rationalist, because he may differ from us on such questions as these!"

(b). Article in the *Presbyterian Review*, 1881, on "The Right, Duty, and Limits of Biblical Criticism" (pp. 552, 579), which was used in *Biblical Study* in 1884 (pp. 138, 242, 243).

(c). Article on "Biblical Theology" in the *Presbyterian Review*, 1882 (pp. 516, 527), which was taken up into *Biblical Study* in 1884, as Chapter XI. (pp. 387, 404.)

(d). The *Holy Scriptures a Means of Grace*, address before the Sunday-school teachers of the Presbytery of New York in 1883, repeated before the Reformed Theological Seminary at Lancaster, Pa., and published as Chapter XII. of *Biblical Study* in 1884.

I read from pages 411–412:

"The Inspiration of the Word of God is a highly important doctrine, but it must not be so greatly emphasized as to lead us to neglect other and still more important aspects of the Bible. Inspiration has to do with the truthfulness, reliability, accuracy, and authority of the Word of God; the assurance that we have that the instruction contained therein comes from God. But these attributes of the divine Word that we have just mentioned in Biblical terms are deeper and more important than Inspiration. They lie at the root of Inspiration, as among its strongest evidences. They stand out as the most prominent features of the Gospel, independent of the doctrine of Inspiration. They are features shared by the Bible with the Church and the Sacraments which are not inspired and are not infallible. They are those attributes that make the Bible what it is in the life of the people and the faith of the church without raising the question of Inspiration. They ascribe to the Word of God a divine power (δύναμις) such as is contained in a seed of life, the movement of the light, the activity of a sword, a power that works redemption, the supreme means of grace."

Also from pages 416–417:

"The Scriptures are means of grace because they have in

them the grace of God in Jesus Christ, the grace of regeneration and sanctification. In what, then, lies the *efficacy* of this
grace? How are we regenerated and sanctified by the word of
redemption in Christ? 'The Spirit of God maketh the reading,
but especially the preaching of the Word, an effectual means of
enlightening, convincing, and humbling sinners, of driving them
out of themselves, and drawing them unto Christ; of conform-
ing them to his image, and subduing them to his will; of
strengthening them against temptations and corruptions; of
building them up in grace, and establishing their hearts in holiness and comfort through faith unto salvation.' These are faithful and noble words. They ought to become more real to the
experience of the men of this generation, where the peril, on the
one hand, is in laying too much stress on doctrines of faith, and,
on the other, in overrating maxims of morals. Religion, the experience of the divine grace and growth therein, is the chief
thing in the use of the Bible and in Christian life. The Holy
Scriptures are means of grace, but means that have to be applied
by a divine force to make them efficacious. There must be an
immediate contact and energetic working upon the readers and
hearers and students of the Word by a divine power. The Word
of God does not work *ex opere operato*—that is, by its mere use.
It is not the mere reading, the mere study of the Bible, that is
efficacious. It is not the Bible in the house or in the hands. It
is not the Bible read by the eyes and heard by the ears. It
is not the Bible committed to memory and recited word for
word. It is not the Bible expounded by the teacher and ap-
prehended by the mind of the scholar. All these are but external forms of the Word which enwrap the spiritual substance,
the grace of redemption. The casket contains the precious
jewels. It must be opened that their lustre and beauty may
charm us. The shell contains the nut. It must be cracked or
we cannot eat it. The pitcher contains the water; but it must be
poured out and drunk to satisfy thirst. The Word of God is
effectual only when it has become dynamic, and wrought vital
and organic changes, entering into the depths of the heart,
assimilating itself to the spiritual necessities of our nature,
transforming life and character. This is the purpose of the grace
which the Bible contains. This is the power of grace that the
Bible exhibits, in holding forth to us Jesus Christ the Saviour.

This can be accomplished in us only by the activity of the Holy Spirit working in and through the Scriptures in their use."

(e). Article, "A Critical Study of the History of the Higher Criticism," in the *Presbyterian Review*, 1883. I read from pages 129–130:

"We have not one narrative, but a fourfold narrative of the origin of the old covenant religion coming down to us from the Mosaic age, as we have a fourfold gospel giving the narrative of the origin of the new Covenant religion. There is, indeed, a remarkable correspondence in these four types or points of view. The second Elohist may be compared to Mark, the Jehovist with Matthew, the first Elohist with Luke, and the Deuteronomist with John. The difference between the Pentateuch and the gospels is that the four narratives of the Pentateuch have been compacted by an inspired Redactor; whereas the gospels have to be harmonized by uninspired teachers in the Church. How this unity in variety strengthens the credibility of the Pentateuch! As the four gospels contain the gospel of Christ, so the narratives of the Pentateuch contain the law of Moses. As our Saviour is set forth by the evangelist as the mediator of the new covenant, Moses is set forth by the narratives of the Pentateuch as the mediator of the old covenant.

"(2). The Pentateuch does not give us one Mosaic code, but three codes of Mosaic legislation, a judicial code, a people's code, and a priest-code, contained in the Jehovistic, Elohistic, and Deuteronomic narratives, somewhat as the gospels present us the discourses of Jesus in the varied types peculiar to Matthew, to Luke, and to John."

(f). Address at the beginning of the term of Union Theological Seminary, September, 1883, on Interpretation of Holy Scripture, published as Chapter X. of *Biblical Study*, in 1884. I read from page 359:

"The rationalists sink the unity in the variety; the scholastics destroy the variety for the sake of the unity. The true evangelical position is, that the Bible is a vast organism in which the unity springs from an amazing variety. The unity is not that of a mass of rocks or a pool of water. It is the unity that one finds in the best works of God. It is the unity of the ocean where every wave has its individuality of life and movement. It is the unity of the continent, in which mountains and rivers, valleys and uplands, flowers and trees, birds and insects, animal and human life combine to distinguish it as a magnificent whole from other continents. It is the unity of the heaven, where star differs from star in form, color, order, movement, size, and importance, but all declare the glory of God."

And also 365–366:

" It was this principle, 'that the supreme judge, by which all controversies of religion are to be determined, and all decrees of councils, opinions of ancient writers, doctrines of men, and private spirits are to be examined, and in whose sentence we are to rest, can be no other but the Holy Spirit speaking in the Scripture,' that made the Puritan faith and life invincible.

"O that their descendants had maintained it! If they had laid less stress upon the minor matters—the order of the decrees, the extent of the atonement, the nature of imputation, the mode of inspiration, and the divine right of presbytery,—and had adhered to this essential principle of their fathers, the history of Puritanism would have been higher, grander, and more successful. We would not now be threatened with the ruin that has overtaken all its unfaithful predecessors in their turn. Let their children return to it; let them cling to it as the most precious achievement of British Christianity; let them raise it on their banners, and advance with it into the conflicts of the day; let them plant it on every hill and in every valley throughout the world; let them not only give the Bible into the hands of men and translate it into their tongues, but let them put it into their hearts, and translate it into their lives. Then will Biblical interpretation reach its culmination in practical interpretation, in the experience and life of mankind."

(g). *Biblical Study*, first edition, 1884, second, third, and fourth editions in subsequent years. I read from pages 136–137:

" The principles on which the canon of Scripture is to be determined are, therefore, these: (1). The testimony of the church, going back by tradition and written documents to primitive times, presents probable evidence to all men that the Scriptures, recognized as of divine authority and canonical by such general consent, are indeed what they are claimed to be.

"(2). The Scriptures themselves, in their pure and holy char-acter, satisfying the conscience ; their beauty, harmony, and majesty satisfying the æsthetic taste ; their simplicity and fidelity to truth, together with their exalted conceptions of man, of God, and of history, satisfying the reason and the intellect ; their piety and devotion to the one God, and their revelation of redemption, satisfying the religious feeling and deepest needs of mankind—all conspire to more and more convince that they are indeed sacred and divine books.

"(3). The Spirit of God bears witness by and with the particu-lar writing, or part of writing, in the heart of the believer, removing every doubt and assuring the soul of its possession of the truth of God, the rule and guide of the life.

"(4). The Spirit of God bears witness by and with the several writings in such a manner as to assure the believer in the study of them that they are the several parts of one complete divine revelation, each writing having its own appropriate and indis-pensable place and importance in the organism of the canon.

"(5). The Spirit of God bears witness to the church as an organized body of such believers, through their free consent in various communities and countries and centuries, to this unity and variety of the Scriptures as the one complete and perfect canon of the divine word to the church.

"And thus the human testimony, the external evidence, attains its furthest possible limit as probable evidence, bringing the inquirer to the Scriptures with a high and reverent esteem of them, when the internal evidence exerts its powerful influence upon his soul, and at length the divine testimony lays hold of his entire nature and convinces and assures him of the truth of God and causes him to share in the consensus of the Christian church."

And also on page 222 :

"There are large numbers of the biblical books that are *anonymous: e. g.*, the Pentateuch, Joshua, Judges, Samuel, Kings,

Chronicles, Ezra, Nehemiah, Esther, Job, Jonah, Ruth, many of the Psalms, Lamentations, and the epistle to the Hebrews.

"Tradition has assigned authors for all of these. It is also maintained that the internal statements of some of these books point to their authorship by certain persons. These latter are questions of interpretation. The vast weight of the Biblical scholarship of the present day is, however, with reference to the books mentioned above, against any such interpretation of them as discovers authorship in their statements. Such interpretation is forced, and is regarded as based on preconceptions and dogmatic considerations."

Also on pages 227–228:

"It is now conceded by most critics that the Pentateuch is composed of four separate historical narratives, each with its code of legislation, and that these have been compacted into their present form by one or more editors. The *Baba Bathra* makes Moses the editor or author of the Pentateuch. If the inspiration of the Pentateuch depends upon the sole Mosaic authorship, then criticism has come into irreconcilable conflict with its inspiration. But this is only a presumption of tradition. The inspiration and authority of the Pentateuch are as safe, yes, safer, with the view that these books were compiled, as were the other historical books of the Old Testament. The question as to the authenticity of the Bible is whether God is its author; whether it is inspired. This cannot be determined by the higher criticism in any way, for the higher criticism has only to do with human authorship, and has nothing to do with the divine authorship, which is determined on different principles, as we have seen in our study of the canon."

And also on pages 240–241:

"There are chronological, geographical, and other circumstantial inconsistencies and errors which we should not hesitate to acknowledge. These errors arise in the department of exegesis more than in higher criticism. It does not follow, however, that circumstantial, incidental errors, such as might arise from the inadvertence of lack of information of an author, are any impeachment of his credibility. If we distinguish between revelation and inspiration, and yet insist upon inerrancy with reference to the latter as well as the former, we virtually do away with the distinction; for no mere man can escape altogether human errors unless divine revelation set even the most familiar things in a new and infallible light, and also so control him that he cannot make a slip of the eye or the hand, a fault in the imagination, in conception, in reasoning, in rhetorical figure, or in grammatical expression; and indeed so raise him above his fellows that he shall see through all their errors in science and philosophy as well as theology, and anticipate the discoveries in all branches of knowledge by thousands of years. Errors of inadvertence in minor details, where the author's position and character are well known, do not destroy his credibility as a witness in any literature or any court of justice. It is not to be presumed that divine inspiration lifted the author above his age any more than was necessary to convey the divine revelation and the divine instruction with infallible certainty to mankind."

(*h*). *American Presbyterianism*, published in 1885. I read from pages 9–11:

"Presbyterianism has been too often represented by spurious types which were not born of Presbyterianism, but were the children of Anabaptism. The Presbyterian principle recognizes the supremacy of the Holy Spirit in the Scriptures, but declines to imprison his divine energy in its external form and letter. Presbyterianism did not reject the authority of the papal church and the prelatical church, in order to establish the authority of a Presbyterian church. It did not make the Bible supreme as a book, but as the living word of the living God. It did not bind itself to a *written* book, but to the Holy Spirit, who uses the Bible (written or spoken) as a means of grace. Presbyterianism recognizes the enthroned Christ as the source of Christianity to every age. The Word of God is the 'sceptre of his kingdom,' and divinely called presbyters are his officers, commissioned to govern the church with his authority and in his fear.

"It never was a legitimate Presbyterian principle to confine worship, doctrine, and practice to the express command of Scripture. It was a perversion of the Presbyterian principle which required a 'Thus saith the Lord' for every precept and every practice. This was a mark of the separating Anabaptists and Brownists, and not of the Presbyterians. Presbyterians follow not only what is 'expressly set down in Scripture,' but also what 'by good and necessary consequence may be deduced from Scripture.' The teachings of Scripture are far-reaching and vastly comprehensive.

"We acknowledge the inward illumination of the Spirit of God to be necessary for the saving understanding of such things as are revealed in the Word ; and there are some circumstances concerning the worship of God and government of the Church, common to human actions and societies, which are to be ordered by the light of nature and Christian prudence, according to the general rules of the Word, which are always to be observed." (Westminster Confession, I., 6.)

"The Holy Spirit guides in the application of the principles of Scripture to all the circumstances of Christianity in the successive ages of the Church. The light of nature and Christian prudence do not conflict with the teaching of Scripture, but take their place in subordination to the voice of the Spirit in the Scripture, and co-operate for the establishment of Christianity in the world. Those who refuse to recognize the use of the light of nature and Christian prudence in the circumstantials of religion, and restrict Presbyterian order and worship and life to the *express* words of Scripture, have abandoned Presbyterian principles, and have gone over to the side of the separating Anabaptists and Brownists of the seventeenth century."

(*i*). *Messianic Prophecy*, published in 1886. I read from page 67 as follows :

"The analysis of the Pentateuch into four distinct narratives, with their distinct codes of legislation, is the result of a century of study by the most famous critics of the age. There are slight differences of opinion in the analysis at some points; but these are chiefly at the seams which bind the narratives together, and are due to the editor's work, who in his efforts to make the entire composition as harmonious and symmetrical as possible, sometimes obscured the signs of difference. But the concord of critics in the work of analysis as a whole is wonderful, in view of the difficulties that beset the work of higher criticism.   The few objectors among Hebrew scholars display their own familiarity with the practical work of criticism when they overlook these solid results and point to the difficulties as evidences that the problem has not been solved.   The differences of opinion among practical critics, and the difficulties in the analysis, are where they ought to be from the very nature of the case.   Instead of disproving the work of criticism, they are therefore an indirect evidence of its correctness.   The differences and difficulties disappear one after another as the investigation advances.   The evidences for the analysis into four narratives are—(1) Differences in use of words and phrases ; (2) differences in style and methods of composition ; (3) differences in point of view and representations of religious institutions, doctrines, and morals."

Also on page 192 :

" The unity of Isaiah is still stoutly defended by many scholars, who prefer to adhere to the traditional view with all its difficulties, rather than follow the methods of the higher criticism, and accept its results.   The same essential principles are involved in the literary analysis of Isaiah as in the literary analysis of the Pentateuch, the Psalter, and the Book of Proverbs and the Wisdom literature generally.   Tradition has ascribed these groups of writings to the four greatest names in Hebrew literary history.   But literary and historical criticism in all these cases has disclosed groups of writings of different authors and different times.   This literary analysis has disturbed many traditional opinions that seem to have had no other origin than pure conjecture ; but it has enabled us to understand the historic origin of the several writings, has given the key to their correct interpretation, and has shown the wondrous variety of form and content in Hebrew literature.   The development of the inspired literature and theology is now beginning to disclose itself with a wealth of meaning which was unknown to those who in an uncritical age imposed their conjectures upon the word of God, and which escapes those who allow themselves to be blinded by these human conjectures and traditions to the real facts and truths of the Scriptures themselves."

And also page 408 :

" This wondrous prophecy, as it has expanded in three successive editions, finds its only appropriate historical situation in the exile. Looking forward from thence it builds on all the previous prophets, and transcends them all in the bulk and grandeur of its representations. It is related to the Book of Ezekiel as the inner to the outer; as the essential spirit and substance to its formal envelope. It seems to us that Ezekiel could never have written his apocalypse if he had seen or heard of the doctrines of Isa. xl.–lxvi. It is indeed not at all strange that some Jewish Rabbins and some modern scholars have doubted the inspiration of Ezekiel, who differs so greatly from the Mosaic codes on the one side, and from Isa. xl.–lxvi. on the other. The difficulty is resolved only when we see that Ezekiel stands on a lower stage in the development of the Messianic idea than the great unknown, who had Ezekiel and Jeremiah, the exile and the body of ancient prophecy behind him; and thus could grasp the whole doctrine of his predecessors, and rise from it to greater heights of prediction."

(*j*). *Whither?* published in 1889, second and third editions, 1890. I read from page 11 as follows :

" None of the older divines gave the human reason its proper place in religion and theology. They were all too much involved in the older methods of exegesis which sought to prove everything possible from the Bible. It was necessary that there should be a long conflict with Deism in order to eliminate *Natural Theology* as a distinct theological discipline; and then the long conflict with Rationalism in order to establish the place of *Speculative Theology*. The Bible does not war against the truths of nature, of the reason, or of history. It rather concentrates their instruction in its central Revelation.

" The Scriptures shine with heavenly light in the midst of the sources of human knowledge. They cannot be understood alone by themselves. It is probable that the reason why the Scriptures have not been more completely mastered in our time, is that the divine truth revealed in other spheres has not been brought into proper relation with the Scriptures. The Sacred Scriptures are for the whole world and for all time. As man grows in the knowledge of nature, of himself and of history, he will grow in the knowledge of the Scriptures."

And also on pages 285–287:

" The future life has been a blank or else a terror to most Protestants and the comfortable hopes inspired by the New Testament have not been enjoyed. The study of the future state in recent times has exposed the faults of the older dogmaticians. It is shown that the doctrine of a private judgment at death has no support in the Scriptures or the Creeds, and that it obstructed and obscured the doctrine of the *dies irae*, the ultimate judgment of the world. It has shown that the current theology confuses and confounds the hell and heaven of the middle state and the hell and heaven of the ultimate state after the day of judgment, and it has accordingly made the middle state more of a reality to many minds. It has held up the light of Christian ethics and shown that the doctrine of immediate sanctification at death is contrary to the Scripture and the Creeds, and has filled the middle state with ethical contents as a place for Christian sanctification. It has called attention to the fact that Jesus Christ knows of but one unpardonable sin, the sin against the Holy Spirit; and asks what is its significance in view of the middle state. It has revived the doctrine of the Apostles' Creed, of the descent of Jesus into hades, His preaching to the imprisoned spirits and His redemption of souls from the ancient abode of the dead. It has called attention to the inconsistency into which the Church has drifted in the new doctrine of the universal salvation of infants, and has demanded that this doctrine shall be considered in some way, so as to correspond with the Protestant doctrine of the order of salvation. It has so pressed the awfulness of the doctrine of the eternal damnation of the heathen world, exceeding the Christian world by hundreds of millions, that the older doctrine of the damnation of all heathen has been abandoned, and efforts have been made to find some mode of relief by which some or many of the heathen may be saved by the grace of God. All these questions are now in dispute. Men are seeking relief by the doctrine of the extension of redemption into the middle state, by conditional immortality, by annihilation of the wicked, and by reaction to the Roman Catholic doctrine of purgatory. The interest in these questions of the future life is widespread and is increasing. There must be liberty of investigation and room for differences in the transition period through which we are passing. The results will be of in-calculable advantage to the Church—for when the future life has become more real, more certain, more fixed, in the hopes and anticipations of men, this life will gain its significance as a prep-aration and vestibule of the better life to come, Christians will live in hope, expectation, and desire, and this hope will work mightily in the consecration and sanctification of men."

(*k*). Article, "*Redemption after Death*," in the *Maga-zine of Christian Literature*, December, 1889. I read from pages 112–114, as follows:

"But justification by faith belongs to the earlier stages of re-demption. All those who are justified are also sanctified. No one can be ultimately and altogether redeemed without sancti-fication.

"It is necessary that believers should have the indwelling of the Holy Spirit, and that they should be 'more and more quickened and strengthened in all saving graces to the practice of true holiness, without which no man shall see the Lord,' and 'so the saints grow in grace, perfecting holiness in the fear of God.' The doctrine of immediate sanctification is a heresy which has always been rejected by orthodox Protestants.

"The Westminster Confession definitely states : 'This sancti-fication is throughout, yet imperfect in this life.' If imperfect in this life for all believers, there is no other state in which it can be perfected save in the Intermediate State. The Intermediate State is therefore for all believers without exception a state for *their sanctification*. They are there trained in the school of Christ, and are prepared for the Christian perfection which they must attain ere the judgment day.

.   .   .   .

"There are some theologians who persuade themselves that they can believe in the immediate justification and the immedi-ate sanctification of infants, of incapables and of heathen adults, in the change of death, in that supreme moment of transition from this life to the Middle State. Such a theory may be stated in words, but it is inconceivable in fact. What a transformation would take place in the intellectual and moral powers of infants, incapables, and the dark-minded heathen ! Such a metamorphosis is not taught in the Scriptures or the Creeds. It would violate the intellectual and moral constitution of man.

"Those who believe it may claim that all things are possible to God. But it might be said that it is just as possible for God to use the water of Baptism, *ex opere operato*, to work regeneration, as Sacramentarians believe; and it is just as possible that the elements of the Lord's Supper may be changed into the real body and blood of our Lord, as the Roman Catholics believe. These divine transformations are just as possible to God and just as credible to the mind of man as the immediate transformation of a little babe into a perfectly holy man in the image of Jesus Christ; or of the instantaneous accomplishment of the entire *ordo salutis* for an idiot in the very moment of death. All such magical doctrines are subversive of the entire structure of Protestantism. They belong to an age of magic, and have no place in an age of Reason and Faith.

"It was a keen thrust of Möhler that Protestantism without a purgatory must either let men enter heaven stained with sin, or else think of an immediate magical transformation at death, by which sin mechanically and violently falls off from us with the body. Hase justly replied that Protestantism would not accept this dilemma, and that Protestant Theology taught that the divine grace was operative, and men capable of moral development after death. This view is the established opinion in German Theology. Dorner, Martensen, Kahnis, and other divines teach that there must be a growth in sanctification in the Middle State. All Protestants must accept this doctrine or they are sure to be caught in the inconsistency of magical, mechanical, and unethical opinions. This opinion is commonly held by Protestants in Great Britain. Why should Protestants in America lag behind their brethren in Europe? We have been caught in the snares of recent errors. Let us break through the snares and re-establish ourselves in the ancient Christian doctrine of the Middle State.

.   .   .   .

"The doctrine of immediate justification and sanctification at death involves the conceit that the child who dies in infancy a few moments after birth is immediately justified and sanctified, receives saving faith and all the Christian graces in an instant; while his brother, who lives in this world, is not justified until he reaches the age in which he can exercise personal faith, and then he has all the struggles of life to undergo until he reaches the limits of human life without the comforts of sanctification, which he cannot receive until death. If this were so, then blessed are those who die in infancy, and thus outstrip their fellows in the Christian race. Vastly better to be born to die, than to be born to live in this uncertain world. What parent would not prefer to lay all his children in an early grave, assured of their salvation, rather than expose them to the dreadful risks of life and the possibility of eternal damnation?

. . . .

"Regeneration is an act of God, and from its very idea is instantaneous, for it is the production of a new life in man. Regeneration is only one of the terms used in the New Testament to describe this beginning of Christian life. Resurrection is more frequently used. Creation is also employed. Effectual Calling was preferred by the Westminster divines. All these terms indicate a divine originating act. Regeneration is always such, and cannot be otherwise.

"But sanctification is the growth of that life from birth to full manhood, into the likeness of Christ. It is always in this world a growth; it is incomplete with the best of men at death. Does it change its nature then? Shall the little babe, the idiot, the seeker after God among the heathen, the Roman Catholic, the Protestant, and the saints of all ages, all alike in an instant leap over this period of growth, however different their stage of progress may be? Shall a babe become a man in an instant? Shall a savage become a philosopher in a moment? Shall a little boy become a John Calvin, and a John Calvin be conformed to the image of Christ, all at a divine creative word? Then the difference between regeneration and sanctification has disappeared for the vast majority of the redeemed.

"If regeneration and sanctification are one act, how can we distinguish the intervening act of justification? and if regeneration, justification, and sanctification may all be one at death, why not in this life, as the Plymouth Brethren teach? Why was the world turned upside down at the Protestant Reformation in order to discriminate justification by faith from sanctification if, after all these centuries of Protestantism, they are really identical for the vast majority of our race, and are only to be distinguished in those in Christian lands who live to maturity and become true Christians?"

(*l*). *The Bible, the Church, and the Reason*, 1891, consisting of an address at the opening of the term of the Union Theological Seminary, September 19, 1889, on "Biblical History," an address delivered at Wellesley College, and before the American Institute of Sacred Literature, at Chicago, on the "Messianic Ideal," in 1890, and several lectures delivered in the city of New York, and elsewhere, in order to set forth the defendant's views of the Bible, the Church, and the Reason, in 1891. I read from pages 63–64:

" When we say that there are historically three great fountains of divine authority, we do not in the statement either co-ordinate these fountains or subordinate them, or in any way define the relation between them. We state a fundamental fact upon which Christianity as a whole is agreed. If there be a seeming discord, it is due to ignorance, misconception, or misrepresentation. It is conceivable that the three fountains might be regarded as co-ordinate. If any one holds such an opinion, we do not.

" The Christian world is divided into three great parties. The Churchmen have exalted the Church above the Bible and the Reason. The Rationalists have exalted the Reason above the Bible and the Church. The Evangelical party have exalted the Bible above the Church and the Reason ; but no party, so far as we know, has made Bible, Church, and Reason co-ordinate, that is, on the same level, in the same order, of equal, independent authority.

" The Roman Catholic does not deny that God speaks to men through the Reason and the Bible ; but he subordinates the Bible and the Reason to the authority of the Church. Evangelicals do not deny that there is divine authority in the Church and the Reason, but they subordinate Church and Reason to the Bible. A Rationalist may deny that there is divine authority in the Bible or the Church, but all that is essential to Rationalism is the maintenance of the supreme authority of the Reason.

" The relation of Bible, Church, and Reason as seats, sources, fountains, media, channels of divine authority, is one of the most difficult of questions; but that each one of them is in some measure such a seat, source, and fountain, is not an open question in any of the historic churches in Christendom. The concord of Christendom is that the Bible, the Church, and the Reason are the three great fountains of divine authority. The discord of Christendom is as to their relative place and value. It should be the aim of all earnest men to diminish the discord so far as possible by avoiding extreme statements, and by determining carefully how far the three fountains share alike in divine authority and how far each one has certain features which discriminate it from the others.

" The Bible, the Church, and the Reason are the three great fountains of divine authority, and yet we claim that the Bible alone is the infallible rule of faith and practice; the conscience alone speaks the categorical imperative within the man; the Church alone administers sacramental grace. The Bible, the Church, and the Reason are all alike dependent upon the real presence of God in them and with them. God is the only divine authority. The Bible, the Church, and the Reason have divine authority only as the instruments of His sovereign will and as the channels of His gracious pleasure, each having its own especial place and importance in the work of grace."

Also on pages 115-117:

" The Scriptures of the Old and New Testaments were immediately inspired by God, but that inspiration did not make them inerrant in matters of science. They have been kept pure in all ages, so far as their purpose of grace, their message of salvation, their rule of faith and practice is concerned; but they are not inerrant now, and it is not probable that they ever were inerrant in matters of chronology. They are sufficient to give that knowledge of God and of His will which is necessary unto salvation; but they are not sufficient to give that knowledge of astronomy and botany. They are the only infallible rule of faith and practice; but they are not the only infallible rule of agriculture and navigation, of commerce and trade, of war and finance. The Scriptures are pure, holy, errorless, so far as their own purpose of grace is concerned, as the only infallible rule of the holy religion, the holy doctrine, and the holy life. They are altogether perfect in those divine things that come from heaven to constitute the divine kingdom on earth, which, with patient, quiet, peaceful, but irresistible might, goes forth from the holy centre through all the radii of the circle of human affairs and persists until it transforms the earth and man.

"The Bible is the infallible rule of faith and practice. It is such, and no one can make it otherwise. It claims to be such, and it vindicates its own claim. The reader of the Bible will find this out for himself. The authority of God will grasp his heart and conscience with irresistible power. The preaching of the Word accompanied by the divine Spirit will ever continue its blessed work of convicting and converting men, of sanctifying them and redeeming them. The Bible will ever be the counsellor and guide of our race, until the second advent of our Lord. From the Bible new truth will break forth from every generation, to lift men higher and urge them onward in the paths of sanctification. The Bible is the master, the infallible rule, and it will ever continue to break in pieces every other rule of faith and life that men may put in its way. It will ever continue to give new theology, new religious forces, and new, fresher and grander guidance in holy life and conduct to all the successive generations of mankind.

"There are errors in the Bible as there are spots upon the sun. The sun-spots do not disturb the light and heat and chemical action of the great luminary or check his reign over our solar system. They suggest that there are greater mysteries of glorious light and reign beyond our vision. So the errors in Holy Scripture do not in the slightest degree impair the divine authority that shines through it or the reign of grace that is carried on in this world by means of it. They intimate, however, that the authority of God and His gracious discipline transcend the highest possibilities of human speech or human writing; and that the religion of Jesus Christ is not only the religion of the Bible, but the religion of personal union and communion with the living God."

I beg leave to put a copy of this volume in the hands of every member of the Presbytery and to ask them to read it as an exposition of the Inaugural for the people in the matters included in the title. Other passages will be read in the Argument for the defence.

(6). I put in evidence all the authorities cited in my writings "in so far as they bear upon this case," and especially the following:

The Synod of New York and Philadelphia vindicated, Philadelphia, 1765.

Eight Letters of Antony Tuckney and Benjamin Whichcote, London, 1753.

W. G. T. Shedd, *Dogmatic Theology*, 1888.

Orders and Regulations for Field Officers of the Salvation Army, London, 1891.

Ball, *Treatise of Faith*, 1637.

Martineau's *Seat of Authority in Religion*.

Westcott's *Commentary on the Epistle of John*.

Newman's *Apologia*.

A. A. Hodge and B. B. Warfield, Article, *Inspiration*, in *Presbyterian Review*, Vol. II.

John Wallis, *Sermons*, London, 1791.

Schaff, *Church History, The German Reformation*, 1888.

Lyford's *Plain Man's Senses Exercised*, 1655.

Beet, *Commentary on Galatians*.

Schaff, *Commentary on Galatians*.

Lechler, *Commentary on Acts*.

Evans and Smith, *Inspiration and Inerrancy*, new edition, 1892.

Alexander, *Commentary on Acts*.

Delitzsch, *Commentary on Genesis*, new edition, 1887.

A. B. Davidson, *Commentary on Job*, 1884.

Delitzsch, *Commentary on Ecclesiastes*, 1875.

Kirkpatrick, *Commentary on Samuel*, 1884.

Perowne, *Commentary on the Psalter*, sixth edition, 1886.

Wesley's *Sermons*, cxxvi.

Calvin, *Commentaries on the New Testament.*

Westcott, *Commentary on Hebrews*, 1889.

Cotton Mather, *Hades Looked Into*, 1717.

Dorner's *Future State*, edited by Smythe, 1883.

A. F. Mitchell, *The Westminster Assembly*, 1883.

A. H. Strong, *Systematic Theology*, 1886.

Dr. Prentiss' article, *Infant Salvation*, in the *Presbyterian Review*, Vol. IV.

G. P. Fisher, *Nature and Method of Revelation*, 1890.

Lux Mundi, 1890, 1892.

White's *Way to the Tree of Life*, 1647.

Sanday, *Oracles of God*, 1891.

A. B. Bruce, *Kingdom of God*, 1890.

H. B. Smith, *System of Theology*, 1884.

W. G. T. Shedd, Article, *N. Y. Observer*, 1891.

W. H. Green, Article, *N. Y. Observer*, 1891.

Add also the following writers who testify to errors in Holy Scripture, from pp. 215–235 of *The Bible, the Church and the Reason.*

These are the Christian scholars through the centuries who testify that there are errors in Holy Scripture. I submit them in evidence.

(1). *Origen.*

"Quin si de aliis compluribus diligenter quis exquisierit Evangelia de dissonantia secundum historiam, quam singulatim tentabimus pro virili ob oculos ponere, vertigine affectus, vel renuet confirmare Evangelia tanquam vera, et judicio suo sibi eligens quod voluerit, alicui ipsorum Evangeliorum adhaerebit, non audens funditus infirmare de Domino nostro fidem ; vel admittens quatuor esse Evangelia, veritatem ipsorum noń in formis et characteribus corporalibus esse adjunget " (*Com. in Joan. Tomus x. 2. Migne, Patrologia, Greek*, Tom. xiv., *Origen*, Tom. iv. 311).

(2). *Jerome.*

"Hoc Testimonium in Jeremia non invenitur. In Zacharia vero, qui pene ultimus est duodecim prophetarum, quaedam similitudo fertur (Zach. xi.) : et quamquam sensus non multum discrepet ; tamen et ordo et verba diversa sunt. Legi nuper in quodam Hebraico volumine, quod Nazaraenae sectae mihi Hebraeus obtulit ; Jeremiae apocryphum, in quo haec ad verbum scripta reperi. Sed tamen mihi videtur magis de Zacharia sumptum testimonium : Evangelistarum et Apostolorum more vulgato, qui verborum ordine praetermisso, sensus tantum de veteri Testamento proferunt in exemplum"(Matth. xxvii. 9). *Migne,Patr. xxvi.*

(3). *Augustine.*

" 30. How, then, is the matter to be explained, but by supposing that this has been done in accordance with the more secret counsel of that providence of God by which the minds of the evangelists were governed ?   For it may have been the case, that when Matthew was engaged in composing his Gospel, the word Jeremiah occurred to his mind, in accordance with a familiar experience, instead of Zechariah.   Such an inaccuracy, however, he would most undoubtedly have corrected (having his attention called to it, as surely would have been the case, by some who might have read it while he was still alive in the flesh), had he not reflected that (perhaps) it was not without a purpose that the name of the one prophet had been suggested instead of the other in the process of recalling the circumstances (which process of recollection was also directed by the Holy Spirit), and that this might not have occurred to him had it not been the Lord's purpose to have it so written.   If it is asked, however, why the Lord should have so determined it, there is this first and most serviceable reason, which deserves our most immediate consideration, namely, that some idea was thus conveyed of the marvellous manner in which all the holy prophets, speaking in one spirit, continued in perfect unison with each other in their utterances,—a circumstance certainly much more calculated to impress the mind than would have been the case had all the words of all these prophets been spoken by the mouth of a single individual.

The same consideration might also fitly suggest the duty of accepting unhesitatingly whatever the Holy Spirit has given expression to through the agency of these prophets, and of looking upon their individual communications as also those of the whole body, and on their collective communications as also those of each separately. If, then, it is the case that words spoken by Jeremiah are really as much Zechariah's as Jeremiah's, and, on the other hand, that words spoken by Zechariah are really as much Jeremiah's as they are Zechariah's, what necessity was there for Matthew to correct his text when he read over what he had written, and found that the one name had occurred to him instead of the other? Was it not rather the proper course for him to bow to the authority of the Holy Spirit, under whose guidance he certainly felt his mind to be placed in a more decided sense than is the case with us, and consequently to leave untouched what he had thus written, in accordance with the Lord's counsel and appointment, with the intent to give us to understand that the prophets maintained so complete a harmony with each other in the matter of their utterances that it becomes nothing absurd, but, in fact, a most consistent thing for us to credit Jeremiah with a sentence originally spoken by Zechariah?" (*Harmony of the Gospels*, III., 7, 30, in *Select Library of the Nicene and Post-Nicene Fathers*, Augustine's Works, VI., pp. 191–2).

(4). *Luther.*

" In diesem Kapitel ist beschrieben der Ausgang und das Ende beider Reiche, des Judenthums und auch der ganzen Welt. Aber die zween Evangelisten, Matthäus und Marcus, werfen die beide in einander, halten nicht die Ordnung, die Lucas gehalten hat; denn sie nicht weiter sehen, denn dass die Worte Christi geben und erzahlen, bekümmern sich nicht damit, was vor oder nach geredet sei; Lucas aber befleissiget sich, es klärlicher und ordentlicher zu schreiben, und erzählet diese Rede zweimal; eines kürzlich am neunzehnten Kapitel, da er von Zerstörung der Juden zu Jerusalem saget; darnach am ein und zwangigsten von diesen beiden nach einander. . . . . So ferne hat nun Christus von den Juden geredt. Nun hab ich zuvor gesagt, dass Matthäus und Marcus die zwei Ende in einander mengen; daraus es hier schwer ist zu unterscheiden und müssen es doch unterscheiden. Darum merke, dass, was bisher geredt ist, alles dorthin auf die Juden

gehet; aber hier flichtet er nun beides in einander, bricht aber
kurz ab, fraget nicht viel nach der Ordnung, wie die Sprüche, so
Christus gesagt hat, auf und nach einander gehen, sondern lässet
es dem Evangelisten Lucas befohlen sein, will aber so sagen, dass
es vor dem jüngsten Tage auch so gehen werde" (Luther's *Werke*,
Erlangen edition, *Vierzehnter Band*, pp. 319, 324).

"Von diesen dreien Verläugnen Petri haben wir oben gehöret.
Die anderen Evangelisten beschreibens also, als sind sie geschehen in dem Hause Caiphä: Johannes aber beschreibts, als sei
die erste Verläugnung geschehen in dem Hause Hannä, wie
seine Wort lauten: Hannas sandte Jesum gebunden zu dem
Hohen-priester Caiphas. Dieser Text lautet gleich als sei die
erste Verläugnung in dem Hause Hannä geschehen. Solches zu
vereinigen befehle ich den Scharfsinnigen, wie ich oben auch
gesagt habe. Es kann auch wohl sein, dass Johannes nicht also
gnau und eben gehalten habe die Ordnung im Reden; doch
davon itzt nicht weiter." (Luther's *Werke*, *Funfzigster Band*, p.
325.)

"Aber die fragts sichs, erstlich, wie sich die zweene Evangelisten, Matthäus und Joannes, zusammen reimen. Den Matthäus
schreibet, es sei geschehen am Palmentage, da der Herr zu Jerusalem ist eingeritten: hie lautets im Joanne also, als sei es bald
umb die Ostern nach der Taufe Christi geschehen; wie denn das
Mirakel, dass Christus Wasser zu Wein gemacht hat, auch umb
die Ostern geschehen ist, und ist darnach gen Kaupernaum
gezogen. Denn umb der dreier Könige Tage ist er getauft, und
hat er leichtlich ein kleine Zeit verharren können zu Kapernaum
bis auf Ostern, und da angefangen zu predigen, und das gethan
auf Ostern, davon Joannes hie redet.

"Aber es sind Fragen und bleiben Fragen, die ich nicht will
auflösen; es liegt auch nicht viel dran, ohne dass viel Leute sind,
die so spitzig und scharfsinnig sind, und allerlei Fragen auf-
bringen, und davon gnau Rede und Antwort haben wollen.
Aber wenn wir den rechten Verstand der Schrift und die rechten
Artikel unsers Glaubens haben, dass Jesus Christus, Gottes Sohn,
für uns gestorben und gelitten hab, so hats nicht grossen Mangel,
ob wir gleich auf Alles, so sonst gefragt wird, nicht antworten
können. Die Evangelisten halten nicht einerlei Ordnung: was
einer vornen setzet, dass setzet der ander bisweilen hinten; wie
auch Markus von dieser Geschicht schreibet, sie sei am andern

Tage nach dem Palmtage geschehen. Es kann auch wohl sein,
dass der Herr Solchs mehr denn einmal gethan hat, und dass
Joannes das erste Mal, Matthäus das ander Mal beschreibet.
Ihm sei nu wie ihm wolle, es sei zuvor oder hernach, eins oder
zwier geschehen, so brichts uns an unserm Glauben Nichts ab"
(Luther's *Werke, Sechs und vierzigster Band*, pp. 173-4).

"Proinde tecum non possum sentire, quod 3 Reg. VI. sit in-
telligendus numerus pro bonis tantum judicibus. Sed potius
Actor. XIII. putabo depravatum 400 pro 300, ut in meo Chronico
signavi. Quandoquidem et Stephani narratio Act. VII. cedere
debet Mosi Chronico, ut ibidem ostendi. Igitur aliam afferto
conciliationem Pauli Actor. XIII. cum 3 Reg. VI. Tua ista mihi
non satisfacit" (De Wette's *Luther's Briefe, Fünfter Theil*, p. 489).

(5). *Calvin.*

"Stephen saith, that the patriarchs were carried into the land
of Canaan after they were dead. But Moses maketh mention
only of the bones of Joseph (Gen. 13). And Joshua xxiv. (32)
it is reported, that the bones of Joseph were buried, without
making any mention of the rest. Some answer, that Moses
speaketh of Joseph for honour's sake, because he had given express commandment concerning his bones, which we cannot
read to have been done of the rest. And, surely, when Jerome,
in the pilgrimage of Paula, saith, that she came by Shechem, he
saith that she saw there the sepulchres of the twelve patriarchs;
but in another place he maketh mention of Joseph's grave only.
And it may be that there were empty tombs erected to the rest.
I can affirm nothing concerning this matter for a certainty, save
only that this is either a speech wherein is *synecdoche*, or else
that Luke rehearseth this not so much out of Moses as according to the old fame; as the Jews had many things in times past
from the fathers, which were delivered, as it were, from hand to
hand. And whereas he saith afterward, they were laid in the
sepulchre which Abraham had bought of the sons of Hemor, it
is manifest that there is a fault (mistake) in the word Abraham.
For Abraham had bought a double cave of Ephron the Hittite,
(Gen. xxiii. 9), to bury his wife Sarah in; but Joseph was buried
in another place, to wit, in the field which his father Jacob had
bought of the sons of Hemor for an hundred lambs. Wherefore

this place must be amended" (Calvin's *Commentary on Acts vii.* 16).

" *Say not in thine heart, Who shall ascend?* etc. Moses mentions *heaven* and the *sea*, as places remote and difficult of access to men. But Paul, as though there was some spiritual mystery concealed under these words, applies them to the death and resurrection of Christ. If any one thinks that this interpretation is too strained and too refined, let him understand that it was not the object of the Apostle strictly to explain this passage, but to apply it to the explanation of his present subject. He does not, therefore, repeat verbally what Moses has said, but makes alterations, by which he accommodates more suitably to his own purpose the testimony of Moses. He spoke of inaccessible places; Paul refers to those, which are indeed hid from the sight of us all, and may yet be seen by our faith. If, then, you take these things as spoken for illustration, or by way of improvement, you cannot say that Paul has violently or inaptly changed the words of Moses; but you will, on the contrary, allow, that without loss of meaning, he has, in a striking manner, alluded to the words *heaven* and the *sea.*" (Calvin's *Commentary on Romans x.* 6).

" *And worshipped on the top,* etc. This is one of those places from which we may conclude that the points were not formerly used by the Hebrews; for the Greek translators could not have made such a mistake as to put staff here for a bed, if the mode of writing was then the same as now. No doubt Moses spoke of the head of his couch, when he said, עַל רֹאשׁ הַמִּטָּה ; but the Greek translators rendered the words, ' on the top of his staff,' as though the last word was written הַמַּטֶּה. The Apostle hesitated not to apply to his purpose what was commonly received : he was indeed writing to the Jews; but they who were dispersed into various countries had changed their own language for the Greek. And we know that the Apostles were not so scrupulous in this respect, as not to accommodate themselves to the unlearned, who had as yet need of milk; and in this there is no danger, provided readers are ever brought back to the pure and original text of Scripture. But, in reality, the difference is but little; for the main thing was, that Jacob worshipped, which was an evidence of his gratitude. He was therefore led by faith to submit himself to his son " (Calvin's *Commentary* on *Hebrews xi.* 21).

(6). *Baxter.*

"And here I must tell you a great and needful truth, which . . . . Christians fearing to confess, by overdoing tempt men to Infidelity. The Scripture is like a man's body, where some parts are but for the preservation of the rest, and may be maimed without death : The sense is the soul of the Scripture; and the letters but the body, or vehicle. The doctrine of the Creed, Lord's Prayer, and Decalogue, Baptism and the Lord's Supper, is the vital part, and Christianity itself. The Old Testament letter (written as we have it about Ezra's time) is that vehicle which is as imperfect as the Revelation of these times was : But as after Christ's incarnation and ascension, the Spirit was more abundantly given, and the Revelation more perfect and sealed, so the doctrine is more full and the vehicle or body, that is, the words are less imperfect and more sure to us; so that he that doubteth of the truth of some words in the Old Testament, or of some circumstances in the New, hath no reason therefore to doubt of the Christian religion, of which these writings are but the vehicle or body, sufficient to ascertain us of the truth of the History and Doctrine " (*The Catechising of Families*, 1683, p. 36).

(7). *Rutherford.*

" Mr. *John Goodwin* will allow us no foundation of faith, but such as is made of grammers and Characters, and if the Scripture be wrong pointed, or the Printer drunke, or if the translation slip, then our faith is gone : Whereas the meanes of conveying the things beleeved may be fallible, as writing, printing, translating, speaking, are all fallible meanes of conveying the truth of Old and New Testament to us, and yet the Word of God in that which is delivered to us is infallible. 1. For let the Printer be fallible; 2. The translation fallible; 3. The Grammer fallible; 4. The man that readeth the word or publisheth it fallible, yet this hindreth not but the truth itself contained in the written word of God is infallible. . . . . Now, in the carrying of the doctrine of the Prophets and Apostles to our knowledge, through Printers, translators, grammer, pens, and tongues of men from so many ages, all which are fallible, we are to look to an unerring and undeclinable providence, conveying the Testament of Christ, which in itself is infallible and begs no truth, no authoritie either from the Church as Papists dreame, or from Grammer, Characters, Printer, or translator, all these being adventitious and yesterday accidents to the nature of the word of God, and when Mr. *Goodwin* resolves all our faith into a foundation *of Christian Religion* (if I may call it Religion) *made of the credit, learning and authority of men*, he would have *men's learning and authoritie* either the word of God, or the essence and nature thereof, which is as good as to include the garments and cloathes of man, in the nature and definition of a man, and build our faith upon a paper foundation, but our faith is not bottomed or resolved upon these fallible meanes ; . . . . and though there be errours of number, genealogies, &c., of writing in the Scripture, as written or printed, yet we hold providence watcheth so over it, that in the body of articles of faith, and necessary truths, we are certaine with the certainty of faith, it is that same very word of God, having the same speciall operations *of enlightning the eyes, converting the soule, making wise the simple*, as being lively, *sharper than a two-edged sword*, full of divinity, life, Majesty, power, simplicity, wisdome, certainty, &c., which the Prophets of old, and the writings of the Evangelists, and Apostles had " (*A Free Disputation Against Pretended Liberty of Conscience*, Sam. Rutherford, London, 1649, pp. 362– 363, 366).

"May not *reading, interpunction, a parenthesis, a letter, an accent*, alter the sense of all fundamentalls in the Decalogue ? of the principles of the Gospel ? and turn the Scripture in all points (which Mr. Doctour restricts to some few darker places, whose senses are off the way to heaven, and lesse necessary) in a field of Problemes, and turn all beleeving into digladiations of wits ? all our comforts of the Scriptures into the reelings of a Wind-mill, and phancies of seven Moons at once in the firmament ? this is to put our faith and the first fruits of the Spirit, and Heaven and Hell to the Presse. But though Printers and Pens of men may erre, it followeth not *that heresies should be tolerated*, except we say, 1. That our faith is ultimately resolved upon characters, and the faith of Printers. 2. We must say, we have not the cleare and infallible word of God, because the Scripture comes to our hand, by fallible means, which is a great inconsequence, for though *Scribes, Translatours, Grammarians, Printers*, may all erre, it followeth not that an erring providence of him that hath seven eyes, hath not delivered to the Church, the Scriptures containing the infallible truth of God. Say the *Baruch* might erre in writing the Prophesie of *Jeremiah*, it followeth not that the Prophesie of *Jeremiah*, which we have, is not the infallible word of God; if all *Translatours and Printers* did their alone watch over the Church, it were something, and if there were not *one with seven eyes* to care for the Scripture. But for *Tradition, Councells, Popes, Fathers*, they are all fallible means, and so far forth to be beleeved, as they bring Scripture with them" (*A Free Disputation Against Pretended Liberty of Conscience*, London, 1649, pp. 370, 371).

(8). *Van Oosterzee.*

"Errors and inaccuracies, in matters of subordinate importance, are, as we have already seen, undoubtedly to be found in the Bible. A Luther, a Calvin, a Cocceius, among the older Theologians; a Tholuck, a Neander, a Lange, a Stier, among the more modern ones, have admitted this without hesitation. But this proves absolutely nothing against the truth and authority of the Word, where it is speaking of the Way of Salvation " (*Christian Dogmatics*, Van Oosterzee, p. 205).

(9). *Marcus Dods, Professor of New Testament Exegesis, New College (Presbyterian), Edinburgh.*

"In Scripture we have the infallible truth about God and His salvation. This position is the mean between two equally untenable positions; it is, on the one hand, impossible to maintain the infallibility of Scripture on the ground of its literal accuracy; and, on the other hand, it is impossible to maintain that the Bible is not infallible because there may be found in it inaccuracies. Its infallibility attaches to its main substance and central message. It infallibly achieves the object for which it was designed " (*Magazine of Christian Literature*, Feb., 1892, p. 396).

(10). *William Sanday, Dean Ireland Professor of Exegesis, Oxford.*

"History is strewn with warnings as to the mistakes in which we are involved the moment we begin to lay down what an Inspired Book ought to be and what it ought not to be. I spoke of some of these mistakes last time. They are all so many applications of the assumption that an Inspired Book must be infallible, not merely as a Revelation, but as a Book. Is there any better reason for this than there was for those other assumptions which Bishop Butler showed to be so untenable—that a revelation from God must be universal, that it could not be confined to an obscure and insignificant people; that a revelation from God must be clear—that it could not be wrapt up in difficulties of interpretation; that its evidence must be certain and such as should leave no room for doubt? All these criteria had been actually put forward; the Christian revelation had been tried by them and found wanting. No one would think of putting forward any such criteria now. Yet there is no essential differ-ence between the claim which was then made for the Revelation itself, and the claim which is still made for the Book in which that Revelation is embodied. Such a Book, it is urged, must at the least be infallible. If that were so, we should find it hard to contend with the facts; for the sphere of its infallibility has been steadily narrowed. Its text is not infallible; its grammar is not infallible; its science is not infallible; and there is grave question whether its history is altogether infallible. But to argue thus is to take up a false position from the outset. It is far better not to ask at all what an Inspired Book ought to be, but to content ourselves with the enquiry what this Book, which comes to us as inspired, in fact and reality is. It will not refuse to answer our questions" (*The Oracles of God*, pp. 35-36).

(11). *Alexander B. Bruce, Prof. of Apologetics in the Free Church College (Presbyterian), Glasgow.*

"In conclusion, let us say that men create for themselves a great many difficulties in connection with Scripture by thinking of God too literally as an Author. Viewing the matter abstractly, it is difficult to understand how, if God be really the Author of the Bible, in the sense in which Milton was the author of

Paradise Lost, He should not write in perfect style, and with perfect accuracy in all statements of fact, and in perfect accordance with the ideal standard in morals and religion. He is surely the most consummate Artist; He knows everything; He is absolutely holy. How can He possibly embody His thought in inferior Greek? How can He possibly make a mistake? How can He have anything to do with crude morality or a defective religious tone? To questions of this sort more might be added, such as that one asked by the free-thinker Reimarus, How could God, the Holy One, employ as His agents in revelation men with glaring moral infirmities? There are several ways of dealing with these questions. One is to deny the facts on which they are based: to allege boldly that the Greek is faultless; that there are no mistakes in point of fact, no crude moralities, no religious shortcomings; that all the men of revelation were faultless, saintly, perfectly exemplary persons. Another way is to admit the facts and draw from them the sweeping conclusion, There was no revelation, the Bible is in no sense an exceptional Book. The best way is to admit the facts, and try to discover a way of reconciling them with the reality of revelation and inspiration. This can be done partly by conceiving of God's relation to the Bible as less immediate than was formerly supposed, and partly, and very specially, by giving large prominence to the gracious condescension of God in the whole matter of revelation. Think of God's authorship as spiritual, not literary; and remember that in giving to the world a Bible, through the agency of the best minds in Israel, He was greatly more concerned about showing His grace than about keeping aloof from every form of human imperfection " (*Inspiration and Inerrancy*. Introduction, pp. 34–35).

(12). *Joseph A. Beet, Prof. of Systematic Theology in the Wesleyan Theological College, Richmond, England.*

" Against the foregoing historical arguments, the cursory allusion in Gal. iii. 17 has no weight. About trifling discrepancies between the Hebrew and Greek texts, Paul probably neither knew nor cared. And they have no bearing whatever upon the all-important matter he has here in hand. He adopted the chronology of the LXX., with which alone his readers were familiar;

knowing, possibly, that if incorrect it was only an understatement of the case.

"The above discussion warns us not to try to settle questions of Old Testament historical criticism by casual allusions in the New Testament. All such attempts are unworthy of scientific Biblical scholarship. By inweaving His words to man in historic fact, God appealed to the ordinary laws of human credibility. These laws attest, with absolute certainty, the great facts of Christianity. And upon these great facts, and on these only, rest both our faith in the Gospel and in God and the authority of the Sacred Book. Consequently, as I have endeavored to show in my *Romans*, Diss. i. and iii., our faith does not require the absolute accuracy of every historical detail in the Bible, and is not disturbed by any error in detail which may be detected in its pages. At the same time, our study of the Bible reveals there an historical accuracy which will make us very slow to condemn as erroneous even unimportant statements of Holy Scripture. And, in spite of any possible errors in small details or allusions, the Book itself remains to us as, in a unique and infinitely glorious sense, a literary embodiment of the Voice and Word of God" (*St. Paul's Epistle to the Galatians*, p. 90).

(13). *A. H. Charteris, Prof. of Biblical Criticism in the University of Edinburgh.*

"Errors, as a matter of fact, are admitted by good men on all sides to exist in the books as we now have them, due in most cases to the slips of copyists, but yet such that we have no means of removing them. The fact that good men on both sides admit the existence of such errors, and yet maintain the supreme authority of Scripture, may warn us to beware of dogmatism on either side. It may teach us to shrink from the fierce consistency of the advocates of verbal dictation, without driving us to manifest the arrogance of those who cut and carve in Holy Writ as they think fit,—as though their own minds were the highest of all revelation,—as though they were sure of this one thing only, that there is neither miracle nor marvel in the collection of documents which have 'turned the world upside down'" (*The Christian Scriptures*, pp. 45, 46).

(14). *Alfred Plummer, Master of University College, Durham.*

"The difference, if there be any, between the duration of the drought, as stated here and by St. Luke (iv. 25), and as stated in the Book of the Kings, will not be a stumbling-block to any who recognize that inspiration does not necessarily make a man infallible in chronology. Three and a half years (=42 months= 1,260 days) was the traditional duration of times of great calamity (Dan. vii. 25; xii. 7; Rev. xi. 2, 3; xii. 6, 14; xiii. 5).

. . . . "Have we any right to assume that there was this special Divine care to produce a particular wording, when it is quite manifest that there has not been special Divine care to preserve a particular wording?

"The theory of verbal inspiration imports unnecessary and insuperable difficulties into the already sufficiently difficult problem as to the properties of inspired writings. It maintains that 'the line can never rationally be drawn between the thoughts and words of Scripture'; which means that the only inspired Word of God is the original Hebrew and Greek wording, which was used by the authors of the different books in the Bible. Consequently all who cannot read these are cut off from the inspired Word; for the inspired thoughts are, according to this theory, inseparably bound up with the original form of words. But if it is the thought, and not the wording, that is inspired, then the inspired thought may be as adequately expressed in English or German as in Hebrew or Greek. It is the inspired thought, no matter in what language expressed, which comes home to the hearts and consciences of men, and convinces them that what is thus brought to them by a human instrument is indeed in its origin and in its power Divine. 'Never *man* thus spake' was said, not of the choice language that was used, but of the meaning which the language conveyed.

. . . . "St. Jude probably believed the story about the dispute between Michael and Satan to be true; but even if he knew it to be a myth, he might nevertheless readily use it as an illustrative argument, seeing that it was so familiar to his readers. If an inspired writer were living now, would it be quite incredible that he should make use of Dante's *Purgatory* or Shakespeare's *King Lear?* Inspiration certainly does not preserve those who possess it from imperfect grammar, and we cannot be certain that it preserves them from other imperfections which have nothing to do with the truth that saves souls. Besides which, it may be merely our prejudices which lead us to regard the use of legendary material as an imperfection. Let us reverently examine the features which inspired writings actually present to us, not hastily determine beforehand what properties they *ought* to possess. We not unnaturally fancy that when the Holy Spirit inspires a person to write for the spiritual instruction of men throughout all ages, He also preserves him from making mistakes as to the authenticity of writings of which he makes use, or at least would preserve him from misleading others on such points ; but it does not follow that this natural expectation of ours corresponds with the actual manner of the Spirit's working. ‘ We follow a very unsafe method if we begin by deciding in what way it seems to us most fitting that God should guide His Church, and then try to wrest facts into conformity with our preconceptions ’ (Salmon, *Introduction to the N. T.*, 4th ed., Murray, [1889], p. 528 ”).—*St. James and St. Jude*, pp. 344, 405–6, 424–5.

(15). *Charles Gore, Principal of Pusey House, Oxford.*

“ Here then is one great question. Inspiration certainly means the illumination of the judgment of the recorder. ‘ By the contact of the Holy Spirit,’ says Origen, ‘ they became clearer in their mental perceptions, and their souls were filled with a brighter light.’ But have we any reason to believe that it means, over and above this, the miraculous communication of facts not otherwise to be known, a miraculous communication such as would make the recorder independent of the ordinary processes of historical tradition? Certainly neither S. Luke's preface to his Gospel, nor the evidence of any inspired record, justifies us in this assumption. Nor would it appear that spiritual illumination, even in the highest degree, has any tendency to lift men out of the natural conditions of knowledge which belong to their time. Certainly in the similar case of exegesis, it would appear that S. Paul is left to the method of his time, though he uses it with inspired insight into the function and meaning of law and of prophecy as a whole. Thus, without pronouncing an opinion, where we have no right to do so, on the critical questions at present under discussion, we may maintain with considerable assurance that there is nothing in the doctrine of inspiration to prevent our recognizing a considerable idealizing element in the Old Testament history " (*Lux Mundi*, p. 354).

" The Church is not restrained, in the first place, by having committed herself to any dogmatic definitions of the meaning of inspiration. It is remarkable indeed that Origen's almost reckless mysticism, and his accompanying repudiation of the historical character of large parts of the narrative of the Old Testament, and of some parts of the New, though it did not gain acceptance, and indeed had no right to it (for it had no sound basis), on the other hand never roused the Church to contrary definitions. Nor is it only Origen who disputed the historical character of parts of the narrative of Holy Scripture. Clement, before him in Alexandria, and the mediæval Anselm in the West, treat the seven days' creation as allegory and not history. Athanasius speaks of paradise as a ' figure.' A mediæval Greek writer, who had more of Irenæus than remains to us, declared that ' he did not know how those who kept to the letter and took the account of the temptation historically rather than alle-gorically, could meet the arguments of Irenæus against them.' Further than this, it cannot be denied that the mystical method, as a whole, tended to the depreciation of the historical sense, in comparison with the spiritual teaching which it conveyed. In a different line, Chrysostom, of the literal school of inter-preters, explains quite in the tone of a modern apologist, how the discrepancies in detail between the different Gospels, assure us of the independence of the witnesses, and do not touch the facts of importance, in which all agree.

" The Church is not tied then by any existing definitions. We cannot make any exact claim upon any one's belief in regard to inspiration, simply because we have no authoritative definition to bring to bear upon him " (*Lux Mundi*, pp. 357–8).

(16). *Alfred Cave, Principal of Hackney College, London.*

" So long as the Bible convinces the practical man, to say nothing of the diligent student of its pages, of its unique divine origin, its unique prophecy, its unique apostolic teaching, its unique Gospel, what matters it whether the Bible is wholly iner-rant or not? *Absolute inerrancy, in such a case, is really a some-*

what scholastic and indifferent matter. He who has used as the messengers of His grace so many generations of preachers (who certainly have not been wholly perfect), may surely if He will reveal Himself to men by many generations of writers (who, although specially selected and adapted for their purpose, may yet be not wholly inerrant). Does not the supreme authority of the Bible lie in the revelations recorded rather than in the inspiration which rendered the record possible? And if the revelations are accurate enough for all practical purposes, what matters it whether they are absolutely inerrant?

"Indeed, I cannot help thinking that this doctrine of absolute inerrancy, like the doctrine of papal infallibility, is an outcome of faithlessness, and even of want of courage. We must, we think, put our human defences around the ark of God, or we would make the pursuit of truth easy. But God wills, it would seem, that the path to truth should not be easy, and should be a constant exercise of faith, and God wills, apparently, to demonstrate the reliableness of His Word, in His own way, by the *testimonium Spiritus Sancti*" (*The Homiletic Review*, Feb., 1892, p. 105).

(17). *James Iverach, Prof. of Apologetics, Free College (Presbyterian), Aberdeen.*

"Even when we grant the results, or all the legitimate results of the critical movement, give to criticism all the rights it can claim, we have still all the mighty resources of arguments of the kind we have outlined, wherewith to vindicate the Divine authority and inspiration of the Scriptures, and their claim to be the Word of God and to be the guide and inspirer of men. But this is an argument which can scarcely be used by men who tie us to the formal discussion of a theme which limits itself to the question : Are there or are there not errors in the Scriptures?

. . . . "When we have so many claims to make on behalf of the Word of God, claims which can neither be weakened nor denied, why should we put in the forefront of the battle a claim to errorless perfection, which can only be made good at the cost of endless argumentation, often of the kind which is only special pleading at the best?" (*The Thinker*, Jan., 1892, pp. 27-8).

(18). *Joseph Henry Thayer, Prof. of New Testament Criticism in Harvard University.*

"The view of the Scriptures here urged I have called a 'change.' But let me remind you again that it is such only in reference to current and local and comparatively recent views. Of the great mass of Christian believers down through the centuries it is doubtful whether more than a small fraction have held the hard and fast theory currently advocated among us to-day. They may be said to have been unanimous and emphatic from the first in asserting the inspiration of the written word; but as to the degree and nature of this inspiration there has been great diversity, or at least indefiniteness, among leading Christian thinkers all along. It was not before the polemic spirit became rife in the controversies which followed the Reformation that the fundamental distinction between the 'Word of God' and the record of that word became obliterated, and the pestilent tenet gained currency that the Bible is absolutely free from every error of every sort" (*The Change of Attitude Towards the Bible*, pp. 62–3).

(19). *W. R. Huntington, Rector of Grace Church, N. Y.*

"The advantage gained by shifting the burden of argument from inspiration to revelation is further evident when we consider that inspiration is a thing of degrees, a matter of more and less, whereas, with respect to revelation all we have to ask is, Has it or has it not occurred? There is a sense of the word in which inspiration is credited to all men who accomplish more than the common. Bezaleel is said in the Book of Exodus, to have been filled with the Spirit of God 'to work in gold and in silver and in brass, and in cutting of stones to set them, and in carving of timber.' This is a definition of inspiration large enough to cover the case of Leonardo da Vinci, the Bezaleel of the Renaissance. So then, if Christians confine themselves to a claim of 'inspiration' for the authors of Scripture, they may find men putting the Bible on the same shelf with other sacred books, wedging it in between Plato and Confucius, and quite content to claim for Isaiah and St. Paul only such a measure of the Spirit as they are willing to concede to Dante, Bunyan, and à-Kempis. A revelation, on the other hand, does not admit of degrees.

Either it has been made or it has not been made; either the heavens have been opened and God has showed us the truth, or they are brass over our head for ever.

"To a mind studying the Bible from the point of approach now indicated, many of the so-called difficulties of faith shrink into insignificance. The intimation, for example, of little inaccuracies in the record, whether of an historical, a geographical, or a scientific sort, cease to alarm. Are the great structural lines of the whole fabric right and true? is the real question. Because I accept the erratum of some chronologist who has discovered a wrong date in the Book of Chronicles, it does not follow that I am logically bound to welcome with open arms a whole troop of interpreters who are bent on writing the Resurrection down a myth, and distilling the personality of God into a figure of speech.

. . . . "The simple fact of the matter is this: modern research is modifying,—some say revolutionizing, but it is more accurate to say modifying, old opinions as to the process by which the various books of the Bible were brought into their present combination, and made into the volume as we have it now. Modern research, be it also observed, is doing what it is doing after a fashion not unlike that in which Sedgwick, Murchison, and Lyell changed our old conceptions of the manner in which the globe was brought to be what to-day it is. But the earth itself is precisely what it was before the geologists began to investigate, and the book we know as the Bible is precisely what it was before the critics began to criticise. And just as there are those of us who while thankfully accepting all that Geology can really prove with respect to the formation of the earth's crust, nevertheless hold fast the old-fashioned faith which expresses itself in the words, 'I believe in God, the Father Almighty, Maker'; so there are those of us, and their number is reckoned by tens of thousands, who while ready cheerfully to concede whatever the best critical scholarship may be able to establish regarding the formation of the Scriptures as an historical process, are not at all shaken in their confidence that as the record of God's revelation of Himself, the Bible, substantially as we have it now, will stand to the end of time" (*The Peace of the Church*, pp. 82–85).

(20). *Thomas G. Apple, Professor of Church History in the Theological Seminary of the Reformed Church, Lancaster, Pa.*

"We feel at once that the Ten Commandments and the Sermon on the Mount are the Word of God in a sense that cannot be claimed for certain other portions of the Scripture. St. Paul might be mistaken in his chronology, counting 430 years from the promise made to Abraham to the giving of the law, and yet this would not affect the inspiration of his teaching in the doctrines of the Christian faith.

" 'But where will you draw the line?' it is said, if you begin to make such distinctions. In answer, we reply, we have seen that in some cases such distinction most assuredly must be made, and all that is required is that common sense and intelligence must be used in interpreting the Scripture. In making a revelation God assumes that it is made to intelligent creatures, and, therefore, He does not reveal science, chronology, etc., subjects that man can acquire a knowledge of by his own research, except incidentally, but confines His revelation to supernatural truth which man could not know of himself.

"It is the province of the Higher Criticism to determine such questions as the authorship and age of the different portions of Scripture and the relative importance and authority of the different sections, just as the lower criticism has to do mainly with the purification of the text. Great fears were entertained when Bengel and others began the study of the text by comparing the different MSS., and when first the thousands of various readings were brought out, many people feared that it would destroy all proper faith in the Bible as the Word of God, but we know now that the result has been healthful. This faith has in nowise been lessened, but it has become more intelligent. And so the Higher Criticism must produce equally good results. What though rationalists use it against the Bible? So did Strauss and Bauer try to invalidate the truth of the New Testament, but their attack only served to bring out a better and stronger defence of the gospel of our Lord. Much yet remains to be learned in reference to the Bible, and the more we learn of it the more impregnable will its position become in the faith of believers in Christianity" (*The Reformed Quarterly Review*, Jan., 1892, pp. 16–17).

(21). *George P. Fisher, Professor of Ecclesiastical History in Yale University.*

" What a stupendous miracle would be involved in imparting this impeccable character to so large a body of historical writings as the Bible contains,—writings which run through so many ages ! Of what avail would it be, unless not only the original writers, but also amanuenses and transcribers, were all to be equally guarded to the end of time ? Exaggerated statements on this subject are the occasion, at present, of two great evils. One mischievous consequence of them is that the truth and divine origin of Christianity are staked on the literal correctness. of even the minutest particulars in the copious narratives of Scripture. The conscientious student, seeing that such views. are untenable in the light of fair historical criticism, is virtually bidden to draw the inference that the foundations of the Christian faith are gone. Moreover, some of the most impressive arguments in defence of historical Christianity, which depend on the presence of unessential discrepancies, showing the absence of collusion, and in various other ways confirming the truthfulness of the main features of the narrative, are precluded from being used whenever the obsolescent theory that the biblical narratives are drawn up with the pedantic accuracy of a notary public is still insisted on. It is a conception of inspiration, it may be added, which the sacred historians themselves do not allege " (*Nature and Method of Revelation*, pp. 41, 42).

(22). *Marvin R. Vincent, Professor of Sacred Literature, Union Theological Seminary, New York.*

" We must construct our formula of inspiration (if we deem it wise to attempt that task at all) from an *actual* and not from an *imaginary* Bible. All that we can do is to study our Hebrew and Greek Bibles in the best texts which critical scholarship can give us, and to see for ourselves whether the contents *are* literally accurate and consistent in date, quotation, and other detail. If, on such examination, we find errors or discrepancies, exegesis compels us to abandon, not the *fact* of inspiration, but *that particular theory* of inspiration, and to seek for another which will agree with the facts."

. . . . "It is difficult to avoid severe expressions concerning the attempts of certain divines, and writers in the religious journals, to stigmatize as unorthodox those who deny the verbal infallibility of Scripture, and to represent them as drawing their arguments from sceptical sources. The question of Christian courtesy, charity, and candor entirely apart, such utterances betray an ignorance which is unpardonable in men who assume to shape and direct public opinion. It ought not to be necessary to inform such that the denial of verbal infallibility is not only no new thing, but that it has been asserted by a host of Christian scholars, of the first rank, since the days of Jerome, not to go farther back" (*Exegesis, An Address*, pp. 11, 40).

(23). *J. H. Fairchild, ex-President of Oberlin College, Ohio.*

"It is impossible to prove absolute inspiration in the sense claimed. The Scriptures do not affirm it, and no other proof is possible. No human wisdom is competent to search it out in the Scriptures, and establish it, in reference to every affirmation. It might be safely claimed that there is marvelous accuracy, even in the geographical and historical statements, and marvelous wisdom in reference to all matters of science—such wisdom as seems to imply divine guidance; securing the use of popular expressions such as are always appropriate, and the avoidance of all technical terms which imply a scientific theory. This claim might be reasonably maintained. But to go farther, and claim the absolute accuracy of all minute statements of fact, or the absolute harmony of all these statements with one another—this is a task which the broadest and most thorough scholarship in Scriptural learning would not undertake. Indeed, such scholars suppose they find minute statements, in the Scriptures, which they cannot reconcile with each other, or with the facts. The advocate of absolute inspiration disposes of these cases by assuming that, if we knew the facts perfectly, the difficulty would disappear. But this is not proved, and cannot be; and absolute inspiration, to avail us as such, must be absolutely proved" (*Inspiration of the Scriptures, Bibliotheca Sacra*, Jan., 1892, p. 20).

I also beg leave to submit, without reading in accordance with the ruling of the Presbytery, the following, which testify against the Mosaic authorship of the Pentateuch, and the Integrity of Isaiah (pp. 236–247 of *The*

VI.

WHO ARE "THE HIGHER CRITICS"?

THE following is a list of the chief modern authorities who hold the modern critical views. Some of these are rationalists, but the majority of them are evangelical Christians. All of them, so far as I know, are honest, faithful, and truth-seeking scholars. They all recognize the composite character of the Hexateuch and Isaiah, though they differ as to the date of the documents and as to the extent and thoroughness with which they make the analysis of the documents. But however much they differ in details, they stand in solid phalanx against the traditional theory that Moses is responsible for our Pentateuch in its present form and that Isaiah wrote the whole of the book which bears his name.

The list is limited to those who have lived during the past 25 years, since 1866, when the writer began his studies in the University of Berlin. Those who have died are marked with a †. We do not propose to give all writers or all the writings of the authors cited; but only the chief writings, and a sufficient number to indicate their critical opinions.

I. Germany.

(1) University of Berlin.

Prof. AUGUST DILLMANN. *Die Genesis.* 5te Aufl. 1886; *Exodus und Leviticus.* 2te Aufl. 1880; *Numeri, Deuteronomium, und Josua.* 2te Aufl. 1886; *Der Prophet Jesaia.* 5te Aufl. 1890.

Prof. PAUL KLEINERT. Hertwig's *Tabellen zur Einleitung in die kanonischen und apokryphischen Bücher des Alten Testaments.* 2te Aufl. 1869; *Das Deuteronomium und der Deuteronomiker.* 1872.

Prof. EBERHARD SCHRADER. De Wette's *Einleitung in die kanonischen und apokryphischen Bücher des Alten Testaments.* 8te Aufl. 1869.

Prof. HERMANN L. STRACK. *Einleitung in das Alte Testament,* in Zöckler's *Handbuch der theologischen Wissenschaften.* 3te Aufl. 1889.

†WILHELM VATKE. *Religion des Alten Testaments.* 1835; *Historisch-kritische Einleitung in das Alte Testament.* 1886.

(2) University of Breslau.

Prof. RUDOLPH KITTEL. *Geschichte der Hebräer* in the *Handbücher der alten Geschichte*. 1888.

†H. GRÄTZ. *Geschichte der Juden.* 1864-70.

(3) University of Halle.

Prof. EMIL KAUTZSCH. *Die Genesis mit äusserer Unterscheidung der Quellenschriften,* with the co-operation of Socin. 2te Aufl. 1891; *Die Heilige Schrift des Alten Testaments übersetzt und herausgegeben.* 1-5 Lieferung. 1890-92.

Prof. EDWARD MEYER. *Geschichte des Alterthums.* 1884; *Kritik der Bericht über die Eroberung Palestinas.* Z. A. W. 1881; *Die Krieg gegen Sichon.* Z. A. W. 1885.

†HERMANN HUPFELD. *Die Quellen der Genesis.* 1853.

†D. KONSTANTIN SCHLOTTMANN. *Kompendium der Biblischen Theologie.* 1889.

†EDUARD RIEHM. *Alttestamentliche Theologie.* 1889; *Einleitung in das Alte Testament.* 1889-1890.

(4) University of Strassburg.

Prof. THEODOR NÖLDEKE. *Die Altestamentliche Literatur.* 1866; *Untersuchungen zur Kritik des Alten Testaments.* 1869.

Prof. KARL BUDDE. *Die Biblische Urgeschichte.* 1883; *Die Bücher Richter und Samuel, ihre Quellen und ihr Aufbau.* 1890; *Die Gesetzgebung der mittleren Bücher des Pentateuchs.* Z. A. W. 1891 (2).

Prof. WILHELM NOWACK. *Der Prophet Hosea.* 1880.

†EDUARD REUSS. *Die Geschichte der Heiligen Schriften Alten Testaments.* 2te Auf. 1890; *La Bible.* Vol. I. 1879.

†AUGUST KAYSER. *Das vorexilische Buch der Urgeschichte Israels und seine Erweiterungen.* 1874.

(5) University of Marburg.

Prof. W. W. BAUDISSIN. *Die Geschichte des Alttestamentlichen Priesterthums.* 1889.

Prof. JULIUS WELLHAUSEN. *Prolegomena zur Geschichte Israels.* 3te Ausg. 1886; *Die Composition des Hexateuchs und der historischen Bücher des Alten Testaments.* 2te Druck mit Nachträgen. 1885; Bleek's *Einleitung in das Alte Testament.* 4te Aufl. 1878; *Sketch of the History of Israel.* Third Edition. 1891.

Prof. ADOLPH JÜLICHER. *Die Quellen von Exodus VII.-XXIV.* in J. P. T. 1882.

(6) University of Giessen.

Prof. BERNHARD STADE. *Geschichte des Volkes Israels.* 1881–88; *Hebräisches Worterbuch zum Alten Testaments*, with Siegfried. 1te Abtheil. 1892.

(7) University of Rostock.

Prof. EDUARD KÖNIG. *Der Offenbarungsbegriff des Alten Testaments.* 1882; *The Religious History of Israel.* 1885.

(8) University of Greifswald.

Prof. FRIEDRICH W. BÄTHGEN. *Beiträge zur Semitischen Religionsgeschichte.* 1888.

Prof. FRIEDRICH GIESEBRECHT. *Der Sprachgebrauch des Hexateuchischen Elohisten* in Z. A. W. 1881 (2); *Beiträge zur Jesaiakritik.* 1890.

(9) University of Göttingen.

Prof. HERMANN SCHULTZ. *Alttestamentliche Theologie.* 4te Aufl. 1885.

Prof. RUDOLPH SMEND. *Der Prophet Ezechiel.* 1880.

†HEINRICH EWALD. *Die Propheten des Alten Bundes.* 2te Ausg. 1867–8; *Commentary on the Prophets.* 1875–81; *Die Lehre der Bibel von Gott oder Theologie des Alten und Neuen Bundes.* 1871; *Geschichte des Volkes Israel.* 3te Ausg. 1864–8; *History of Israel.* 1869–71.

†ERNST BERTHEAU. *Das Buch der Richter und Ruth.* 2te Aufl. 1883; *Die sieben Gruppen Mosäischer Gesetze in den drei mittleren Büchern des Pentateuchs.* 1840.

†PAUL A. DE LAGARDE. *Orientalia*, I. 1879; *Symmicta*, I. 1877; *Mittheilungen*, I. 1884.

(10) University of Leipzig.

Prof. ALBERT SOCIN. *Die Genesis mit äusserer Unterscheidung der Quellenschriften*, with Kautzsch. 2te Aufl. 1891.

Prof. HERMANN GUTHE. *Die Zukunftsbild des Jesaias.* 1885.

Prof. FRIEDRICH DELITZSCH. *Wo lag das Paradies?* 1881.

Prof. FRANTS BUHL. *Jesaja oversat og fortolket.* 1889–1891.

†FRANZ DELITZSCH. *Zwölf Pentateuch-kritische Studien*, Z. K. W. 1880; *Neuer Commentar uber die Genesis.* 1887; *Commentar uber das Buch Jesaia.* 4te Aufl. 1889; *Messianic Prophecy.* 1891.

(11) University of Heidelberg.

Prof. ADALBERT MERX. *Nachwort* in Tuch's *Commentar über des Genesis.* 2te Aufl. 1871.

Prof. LUDWIG LEMME. *Die religionsgeschichtliche Bedevtung des Decalogs.* 1880.

†FERDINAND HITZIG. *Der Prophet Jesaja.* 1833; *Geschichte des Volkes Israel.* 1869; *Vorlesungen über Biblische Theologie.* 1880.

(12) University of Königsberg.

Prof. CARL H. CORNILL. *Das Buch des Propheten Ezechiel.* 1886; *Einleitung in das Alte Testament* in the *Grundriss der Theologischen Wissenschaften.* 1891.

(13) University of Kiel.

Prof. EMIL SCHÜRER. *Geschichte des Jüdischen Volkes.* 2te Aufl. 1886–89.

Prof. AUGUST KLOSTERMANN. *Die Heiligkeitsgesetz* in *Lutherischer Zeitschrift.* 1877; *Beiträge zur Entstehungsgeschichte des Pentateuchs.* N. K. Z., 9, 10.

Prof. CONRAD BREDENKAMP. *Gesetz und Propheten.* 1881; *Der Prophet Jesaia erlautert.* 1886–87.

(14) University of Bonn.

Prof. ADOLPH KAMPHAUSEN. Bleek's *Einleitung in das Alte Testament.* 2te Aufl. 1865; *Das Lied Moses.* 1862.

(15) University of Tübingen.

Prof. JULIUS GRILL. *Die Erzväter der Menscheit.* 1875; *Der achtundsechzigster Psalm.* 1883.

(16) University of Erlangen.

Prof. AUGUST KÖHLER. *Lehrbuch der Biblischen Geschichte.* 1889–90.

(17) University of Munich.

Prof. FRITZ HOMMEL. *Die Semitischen Völker und Sprachen*, I. Bd. 1883.

(18) University of Jena.

Prof. CARL SIEGFRIED. *Hebräisches Wörterbuch zum Alten Testamente*, with Stade, 1st Abtheil. 1892.

Prof. JOHANN G. STICKEL. *Das Hohelied.* 1888.

†Prof. LUDWIG DIESTEL. *Geschichte des Alten Testamentes in der Christlichen Kirche.* 1869. *Der Prophet Jesaia.* 4te Aufl. 1872.

(19) Other Scholars.

JOHN HOLLENBERG. *Die deuteronomischen Bestandtheile des B. Joshua* in the *Stud. und Krit.* 1874.

GEORGE EBERS. *Egypten und die Bücher Moses.* 1868.

GUSTAV KARPELES. *Geschichte der Judischen Literatur.* 1886.

JULIUS LIPPERT. *Allgemeine Geschichte des Priesterthums.* 1883.

MAX DUNCKER. *The History of Antiquity.* 1877.

S. MAYBAUM. *Die Entwickelung des altisraelitischen Priester-thums.* 1880.

JULIUS POPPER. *Der Ursprung des Monotheismus.* 1879.

†KARL HEINRICH GRAF. *Der Prophet Jeremia.* 1862. *Die geschichtliche Bücher des Alten Testaments* in Merx *Archiv.* 1866–68.

†L. HERZFELD. *Geschichte des Volkes Israel.* 1847–57.

These are chiefly the professors in the Old Testament depart-ment in the German universities who have expressed themselves in favor of modern critical views of the Hexateuch and Isaiah. If there is any professor in the Old Testament department of any German university who holds the traditional theory of the Hexa-teuch and the book of Isaiah we do not know his name. He has not spoken his opinion. In 1866 the writer was a student of Hengstenberg, who was a great and influential man, having taught several thousand students in his class-rooms. Hengs-tenberg was supported by Hävernick and Keil. Not one of his students now represents his views in any university in Germany. The writer was convinced by Hengstenberg's methods in his class-room that he was wrong. We know of others who went through the same experience. What Hengstenberg could not accom-plish, it is vain to think that any American or English Old Tes-tament professor can do.

We shall now give the names of authorities in

II. Other Countries of the Continent of Europe.

(1) Switzerland.

(a) University of Basle.

Prof. KONRAD VON ORELLI. *Die Alttestamentliche Weissagungen von der Vollendung des Gottesreiches.* 1882. *Old Testament Prophecy of the Consummation of God's Kingdom.* 1885. *Die Propheten Jesaia und Jeremiah.* 1886. *The Prophecies of Isaiah.* 1889. *Das Buch Ezechiel und die zwolf kleinen Propheten.* 1888. *Theologie des Alten Testaments* in Zöck-ler's *Handbuch der theologischen Wissenschaften.* 1889.

Prof. BERNHARD DUHM. *Die Theologie der Propheten.* 1875.

Prof. KARL MARTI. *Die Spuren der sogenannten Grundschrift des Hexateuchs in der vorexilischen Propheten.* J. P. T. 1880. *Der Prophet Jeremia.* 1889.

(b) **University of Bern.**

Prof. SAMUEL OETTLI. *Die geschichtlichen Hagiographen und das Buch Daniel.* 1889.

(c) **University of Zurich.**

Prof. VICTOR RYSSEL. *De Elohistae Pentateuchi Sermone.* 1878. *Untersuchungen über die Textgestalt und die Echtheit des Buches Micha.* 1887.

(d) **University of Geneva.**

Prof. EDOURD MONTET. *Essai sur les origines des partis Saducien et Pharisien.* 1883. Reviews of Reuss, Vernes, and others, in R. H. R., xv. xxi. xxii.

(e) **University of Lausanne.**

Prof. H. VUILLEUMIER. Articles in the *Revue de Théologie et de Philosophie.* 1882–1883.

(f) **Free Church College, Lausanne.**

Prof. LUCIEN GAUTIER. *Le Mission du Prophète Ezéchiel.* 1891.

(2) **University of Dorpat, Russia.**

Prof. WILHELM VOLCK. *Die Biblische Hermeneutik,* in Zöckler's *Handbuch der Theologischen Wissenschaften,* 3te Aufl. 1889.

(3) **France.**

(a) **The Theological Faculty at Montaubon.**

Prof. CHARLES BRUSTON. *Histoire critique de la littérature prophétique des Hebreux depuis les origines jusqu'à la mort d'Isaie.* 1881 ; *Les quatre sources des lois de l'Exode.* 1883; *Les deux Jéhovistes.* R. T. P. 1885 ; *La mort et la sépulture de Jacob.* Z. A. T.

Prof. FERDINAND MONTET. *Le Deutéronome et la question de l'Hexateuque.* 1891.

(b) **College of France, Paris.**

Prof. ALBERT RÉVILLE. *Review of Kuenen* in R. H. R. xxii.

Prof. ERNEST RENAN. *Histoire du Peuple d'Israel.* 1887–91.

(c) **The High School in the Sorbonne.**

Prof. A. CARRIÈRE. *Review of Kuenen's Hexateuch* in R. H. R. xiii. 206.

Prof. MAURICE VERNES. Article, *Pentateuque,* in Lichtenberger's Encyclopedia, x., p. 447. *Une nouvelle hypothése sur la Composition du Deutéronome.* 1887. *Préces d'Histoire Juive.* 1889. *Essais bibliques.* 1891.

Prof. JAMES DARMSTETTER. *Die Philosophie der Geschichte des Jüdischen Volkes.* 1884. *Les prophètes d'Israel* in R. D. M. 1891.

(d) Other Scholars.

GUSTAVE D' EICHTHAL. *Mélanges de critique Biblique.* 1886.

F. H. KRÜGER. *Essai sur la théologie d'Esaïe,* xl.-lxvi. 1881.

CHARLES PIEPENBRING. *Histoire des lieux de culte et du sacer-doce en Israel.* R. H. R. xxiv. 1, 2. *Théologie de l'Ancien Testament.* 1886.

ALEXANDRE WESTPHAL. *Les sources du Pentateuque.* 1888–92.

L. HORST. *Études sur le Deutéronome.* R. H. R. 1887, 1888, 1891. *Leviticus XVII.–XXVI. und Hesekiel,* 1881.

ISIDORE LOEB. *La littérature des pauvres dans la Bible.* R. E. J. xxiii.

†FRANÇOIS LENORMANT. *The Beginnings of History,* edited by Francis Brown. 1882.

(4) Italy. Institute of Florence.

Prof. DAVID CASTELLI. *La Profezia nella Bibbia.* 1882. *Storia degl' Israelite.* 1887. *La Legge del Popolo Ebreo nel suo svolgimento storico.* 1884.

(5) Holland.

(a) UNIVERSITY OF LEIDEN.

Prof. CORNELIS PETRUS TIELE. *Vergelijkende Geschiedenis der Egyptische en Mesopotamische Godsdiensten.* 1869–72. *Outlines of the History of Religion to the spread of the Universal Religions.* 4th edition. 1884.

Prof. HENRICUS OORT. *The Bible for Learners.* 1878–9.

†ABRAHAM KUENEN. *The Religion of Israel.* 1874–5; *The Prophets and Prophecy in Israel.* 1877. *Hist.-crit. Onderzoek naar het Ontstaan en de Verzameling van de Boeken des Ouden Verbonds.* 2de uitgave. 1885-1889; *The Hexateuch.* 1886.

(b) UNIVERSITY OF UTRECHT.

Prof. J. J. P. VALETON. *Jesaja volgens zijne algemeen als echt erkende Schriften.* 1871. *Beteekemis en gebrink van het word Thorâ in het Oude Testament* in the *Theologische Studien.* 1891.

(c) UNIVERSITY OF GRONINGEN.

Prof. G. WILDEBOER. *Het Ontstaan van den Kanon des Ouden Verbonds.* 1889. *De Pentateuch-Kritik en het Mozaische Strafrecht* in *Tigdschrift von Strafrecht.* 1890-i.

(d) UNIVERSITY OF AMSTERDAM.

Prof. CHANTEPIE DE LA SAUSSAYE. *Lehrbuch der Religions-geschichte.* 2 Bde. 1887-89.

Prof. J. KNAPPERT. *The Religion of Israel.* 1878.

(6) Austria.

Prof. WALTER LOTZ (Evangelical Faculty at Vienna). *Quaestiones de Historia Sabbati.* 1883.

VICTOR FLOIGL. *Geschichte des Semitischen Altertums.* 1882.

III. Great Britain.

The chief British scholars who have expressed modern critical views are :

(1) University of Oxford.

Prof. THOMAS K. CHEYNE. *The Prophecies of Isaiah.* 3d edition. 1884; *Jeremiah, his life and times.* 1888; *The Origin and Religious contents of the Psalter.* 1891.

Prof. SAMUEL R. DRIVER. *Critical Notes on the International Sunday-School Lessons from the Pentateuch.* 1887; *Isaiah, his life and times.* 1888. *Introduction to the Literature of the Old Testament* in the *International Theological Library.* 2d edition. 1892.

(2) University of Cambridge.

Prof. ALEXANDER T. KIRKPATRICK. *The Divine Library of the Old Testament.* 1891.

Prof. W. ROBERTSON SMITH. *The Old Testament in the Jewish Church.* 2d edition. 1892; *The Prophets of Israel and their place in History.* 1882; *Lectures on the Religion of the Semites.* 1889.

Prof. HERBERT E. RYLE. *The Canon of the Old Testament.* 1892.

Prof. VINCENT H. STANTON. *The Jewish and the Christian Messiah.* 1886.

(3) Manchester New College.

Prof. JAMES DRUMMOND. *The Jewish Messiah.* 1877.

Prof. J. E. CARPENTER. *The Book of Deuteronomy,* in the *Modern Review.* 1883.

(4) Wesleyan College, Richmond.

Prof. W. T. DAVISON. *Inspiration and Biblical Criticism.* A Paper read at the London Wesleyan ministers' meeting, March 16, 1891.

(5) Countess of Huntingdon's College, Cheshunt.

Prof. OWEN C. WHITEHOUSE. *Franz Delitzsch and Aug. Dillmann on the Pentateuch.* Expositor, Feb., 1888. *Review of Cheyne's Origin and Religious Contents of the Psalter* in *Critical Review,* Jan., 1892.

(6) United College (Independent), Yorkshire.

Prof. ARCHIBALD DUFF, Jr. *Old Testament Theology.* 1892.

(7) University of Glasgow.

Prof. JAMES ROBERTSON. *The Early Religion of Israel.* 1892.

(8) University of Aberdeen.

Prof. A. R. S. KENNEDY. Articles on *Canon Driver and the Pentateuch,* in the *Expository Times,* Nov., 1891, and Jan., 1892.

(9) Free College (Presbyterian), Edinburgh.

Prof. ANDREW B. DAVIDSON. Articles on Isaiah, xl.–lxvi., in the *Expositor.* 1883, 1884.

(10) Free College (Presbyterian), Glasgow.

Prof. GEORGE A. SMITH. *The Book of Isaiah.* 1890.

(11) Other Scholars.

SAMUEL DAVIDSON. *Introduction to the Old Testament.* 1862–3.

Bishop J. J. STEWART PEROWNE. *The Age of the Pentateuch. Contemporary Review,* 1888, Jan. and Feb.

G. J. SPURRELL. *Notes on the Hebrew Text of Genesis.* 1887.

C. H. H. WRIGHT. *Introduction to the Old Testament.* Third Edition. 1891.

ROBERT F. HORTON. *Inspiration and the Bible.* Third Edition. 1891.

H. A. GILES. *Hebrew and Christian Records.* 1877.

C. G. MONTEFIORE. *Recent Criticism upon Moses and the Pentateuch* in the *Jewish Quarterly Review,* Jan., 1891. *Some Notes on the Effects of Biblical Criticism upon the Jewish Religion. Ibid.* Jan., 1892.

F. W. FARRAR. *The Minor Prophets.* 1890.

C. J. BALL. *The Prophecies of Jeremiah.* 1891.

P. RAY HUNTER. *After the Exile.* 1890.

BUCHAN BLAKE. *How to Read Isaiah.* 1891.

W. E. ADDIS. *The Documents of the Hexateuch translated and arranged in Chronological order, with Introduction and Notes.* 1892.

JOSEPH JACOBS. *Recent Researches in Biblical Archæology; Are there Totem-clans in the Old Testament. Archæological Review,* 1889.

†M. KALISCH. *Historical and Critical Commentary on Genesis,* 1858. *Exodus,* 1855. *Leviticus,* 1867, 1872.

†MATTHEW ARNOLD. *The great prophecy of Israel's Restoration.* Fourth Edition. 1875.

†SAMUEL SHARP. *History of the Hebrew Nation.* Fourth Edition. 1882.

†ARTHUR P. STANLEY. *The Jewish Church.* Seventh Edition. 1877.

†JOHN WILLIAM COLENSO. *The Pentateuch and Book of Joshua Critically Examined.* 1862–79.

IV. America.

(1) Harvard University.

Prof. CRAWFORD H. TOY. *Judaism and Christianity.* 1890. *History of the Religion of Israel.* Third Edition. 1884.

Prof. DAVID G LYON. *Results of Modern Biblical Criticism.* O. T. S. 1883.

(2) Yale University.

Prof. GEORGE T. LADD. *The Doctrine of Sacred Scripture.* 1883.

(3) University of Pennsylvania.

Prof. JOHN P. PETERS. *The Scriptures, Hebrew and Christian.* 1886. *Jacob's Blessing.* J. B. L. 1886. *The Date of Leviticus.* J. B. L. 1888.

Prof. MORRIS JASTROW, Jr. *The Bible in the light of Modern Criticism,* in the *American Hebrew.* 1886.

(4) University of Chicago.

Pres. WILLIAM R. HARPER. *The Pentateuchal Question, Hebraica.* 1888–1890.

Prof. EMIL G. HIRSCH. *Modern Views of the Bible.* A memorial discourse on Professor Kuenen. *Reform Advocate,* Jan., 1892.

(5) Johns Hopkins University.

Prof. PAUL HAUPT. *The Cuneiform Account of the Deluge.* O. T. S. 1884.

(6) Andover Theological Seminary.

Prof. GEORGE F. MOORE. *Tatian's Diatessaron and the Analysis of the Pentateuch.* J. B. L. ix. 1889.

(7) Chicago Theological Seminary.

Prof. SAMUEL IVES CURTISS. *The Higher Criticism: Some of its Results. Independent,* July 30, 1891.

(8) Lancaster Theological Seminary.

Prof. FREDERICK A. GAST. *Pentateuch Criticism: Its History and Present State. Reformed Quarterly Review,* April and July, 1882.

(9) Victoria University, Coburg, Canada.

Prof. GEORGE C. WORKMAN. *The Text of Jeremiah.* 1889. *Messianic Prophecy,* in the *Canadian Methodist Quarterly.* 1890 (2).

(10) Lane Theological Seminary.

Prof. HENRY P. SMITH. *The Critical Theories of Julius Wellhausen,* in the *Presbyterian Review,* III. 2. *Biblical Scholarship and Inspiration.* 1891.

(11) P. E. Divinity School, Philadelphia.

Dean E. T. BARTLETT. *The Scriptures: Hebrew and Christian.* 1886.

Prof. L. W. BATTEN. *The Historical Movement traceable in Isaiah xl.–lxvi.,* in the *Andover Review,* Aug., 1891.

(12) Episcopal Theological School, Cambridge.

Prof. M. L. KELLNER. *The Deluge in the Izdubar Epic and the Old Testament. American Church Review.* 1889.

(13) Union Theological Seminary, N. Y.

Prof. CHARLES A. BRIGGS. *Biblical Study.* Fourth Edition. 1891. *Messianic Prophecy.* 1888. *Whither?* Third Edition. 1890. *Biblical History.* 1889. *The Authority of Holy Scripture.* Third Edition. 1891.

Prof. FRANCIS BROWN. *The New Testament Witness to Old Testament Books.* J. S. B. L. *Is the Higher Criticism Scientific? Homiletic Review,* April, 1892. *Hebrew and English Lexicon of the Old Testament.* Part I., 1892. With the co-operation of S. R. Driver and C. A. Briggs.

(14) **Other American Scholars.**

R. HEBER NEWTON. *The right and wrong uses of the Bible.* 1883. *The Book of the Beginnings.* 1884.

WASHINGTON GLADDEN. *Who Wrote the Bible?* 1891.

BENJAMIN WISNER BACON. *The Genesis of Genesis.* 1892.

JOHN W. CHADWICK. *The Bible of To-day.* 1879.

ADOLPH MOSES. *Nadab und Abihu oder der Untergang der Sauliden.* 1890.

†MICHAEL HEILPRIN. *The Historical Poetry of the Ancient Hebrews.* 1879.

The list of British and American scholars who hold to the documentary theory of the composition of the Hexateuch and Isaiah is quite incomplete, because a large number of Professors who hold these views have not written upon the subject. The number of Professors in the Old Testament department who hold to the traditional theory may be counted on one's fingers. Under these circumstances it ought to be plain to every intelligent person, that the traditionalists are in such a hopeless minority that it is extremely improbable that they will ever be able to overcome the weight of scholarship throughout the world which is so overwhelmingly on the critical side. And even if any one should suppose that there are perils in the methods and results of the Higher Criticism, it is, to say the least, unwise, in view of the enormous literature on the critical side and its influence extending so widely and so rapidly, to risk the authority of the Bible upon the maintenance of the traditional theory, and to assert, as some foolish people do, that the scores of evangelical critics are destroying the Bible.

The great majority of the writings mentioned above have been examined by the author. But for a number of them he has relied upon the testimony of his friends, Profs. Toy, Moore, Henry P. Smith, Peters, Brown, Driver, and Gottheil, who have kindly given him their assistance.

These are submitted without reading, in accordance with the ruling of the Presbytery.

All this evidence, whether read or not read, is filed in so far as it bears upon the case.   C. A. BRIGGS.

VI.

THE EXCEPTIONS TAKEN BY PROF. BRIGGS TO THE NEW MATTER INTRODUCED BY THE PROSECUTION INTO THEIR ARGUMENT IN REBUTTAL.

On December 19th, Prof. Briggs raised the question whether the prosecution had a right of rebuttal, according to the Book of Discipline.

Dr. BRIGGS—Before the prosecution proceeds, I wish to have some rules adopted by the house. It is very evident from the Book of Discipline that they have no right to present any further argument. I may say that I would not myself make this objection were it not necessary as a party. The only provision of the Book of Discipline on this subject is, "And then the parties themselves shall be heard." The prosecution have no right of rebuttal, according to the Book. I make that point, Mr. Moderator, and I shall ask a ruling upon it— that the prosecution have no right of rebuttal, according to the Book. I am perfectly willing to make no objection to their speaking in rebuttal for a reasonable time, provided they ask that privilege of the house, and the house grants it. I am not objecting to the prosecution having a right of rebuttal, if the house gives it to them; but I do object to their assuming that they have a right according to the Book. The prosecution, as you will remember, have insisted on the letter of the law from the beginning. When I have in the course of the argument called your attention to precedents of our courts, they have said, "Oh, we have a new Book of Discipline; we must stick closely to the new Book." Now they are in exactly the fix that they have put me in all the way through. They have asked the pound of flesh, and up to this time you have given it to them. The question now is, whether they shall have the blood also. Now, Mr. Moderator, I ask your ruling as to whether they have that right. If the Moderator decides they have the right, I shall appeal to the house. Then if the house decides in my favor I shall not object to a motion that they have a certain time given them. But I shall ask, to save time, that there shall be a ruling to this effect: that the prosecution be required to limit themselves strictly to rebuttal; that they shall not be allowed to traverse the whole case and bring in a new argument against me, and force me to prepare a reply at this late time, when my strength is well-nigh exhausted and when the patience of this house is well-nigh exhausted. I called upon them, you remember, at the conclusion of their argument, to know if they had anything more to say, and, if so, to say it; so that I might know all there was against me, and might be able to reply to it. And I very much believe, from their procedure in the higher court last May, and from certain other things that they have claimed upon this floor, that they will claim the right to do exactly what they please. That is the right they have claimed all the time, and it is a right which I, as a party, cannot concede at this time. There is one other point, Mr. Moderator, and that is that they shall be distinctly prohibited from using in this rebuttal any material that they have prepared prior to the delivery of my argument. I apprehend that a very large portion of the argument of Dr. Lampe has been prepared for months and months before I appeared in my defense. I claim the justice of this house. I ask no indulgence and no mercy from any one. I ask the justice of this house, that they shall be prohibited from bringing in here at this stage of the argument anything not prepared in answer to my argument here, thus forcing you to go into Christmas week and hold sessions of this court, when we are all exhausted, and when some members of the court must retire and lose their vote in order to save their health or their lives. I claim that it is not just for them to bring in at this stage a long argument which was prepared months and months ago. If, with these restrictions and this understanding, they can be allowed to speak for a limited time, I shall not object; but unless these restrictions are made, I object. I ask you, Mr. Moderator, to please rule on my first point.

The MODERATOR—The Moderator is impelled to decide that the question of order is not well taken, and for these reasons:

First: That the usage in such cases is against the point which is raised.

Second: That usage is based upon the law of the church governing complaints and appeals, which distinctly give us this order of the opening and the closing being on the part of those who present their case—the greater including the less.

Third: That the parties cannot have been said to have been heard until the prosecution has had a full opportunity to present its whole case. It has only presented a part of that case so far. It has taken a very small portion of time compared with that accorded to the defendant. You have heard the defendant patiently and fully, as you should have done; and now, in the view of the Moderator, it is only fair, it is only in accordance with our usage and with the principle of our Book, that the prosecution should be heard fully, but not presenting new matter.

Prof. Briggs then appealed from the decision of the Moderator.

The Moderator was sustained by a majority of the Presbytery.

B.

Exception taken Dec. 21st, 1892.

Mr. MODERATOR AND BRETHREN—I beg leave to take exception to that part of the proceedings of the Presbytery of yesterday, recorded in the stenographer's report, which permitted the Rev. Dr. Lampe, arguing on behalf of the prosecution under the cloak of a rebuttal, to introduce new evidence and new matter, and, in large measure, to reargue the Amended Charges and Specifications apart from and without regard to the Argument of the accused; in that (1) he introduced new evidence without the permission of Presbytery, and without notification to the accused, as follows: Henry B. Smith's sermon on *Inspiration; Presbyterian and Reformed Review,* 1892; Article in the *Congregationalist,* Feb. 21, 1889; *John Ball's Catechism; The Bible Doctrine of Inspiration;* Farrar's *Life of St. Paul,* Homiletical Review, May, 1891; Westcott's *Introduction to the Gospels;* D'Aubigné's *History of the Reformation,* Life of Calvin, Chap. IV.; and also a considerable number of extracts from the Works of Lüther and Calvin.

(2). In that he introduced new matter, as for example, an argument on the metaphysical categories from the usage of Aristotle and Kant; an argument from the use of the Old Testament by Christ and His apostles; an argument from the dynamic theory of inspiration; an argument from the stress laid upon single words of the Old Testament by New Testament writers.

(3). In that he argued in more than three-fourths of his argument against the statements of the Inaugural Address, the Response to the Original Charges, the Lectures on the Bible, the Church and the Reason, and the other writings of the accused, and in not more than one-fourth of it was it an effort in rebuttal of the argument of the accused; namely, Stenographer's Report [a] pp. 1120, 1126, as far as "It is of the utmost importance." [b] p. 1131, beginning with "Dr. Briggs' argument," as far as "It is not our faith," p. 1133. [c] p. 1136, as far as "through the word of God," p. 1137. [d] the reference to Isaiah viii. 20, on p. 1141; [e] and to 1 John v. 10 on pp. 1144-1145; [f] pp. 1147-1152, as far as "We are not raising the question." [g] a brief allusion to my interpretation of the Confession of Faith, I., section 1, on p. 1163. [h] a brief reference to passages cited by me from Luther on p. 1181. [i] and to passages cited by me from Calvin, pp. 1185-6; and of these c, d, h and i may have been written in view of the evidence adduced in *The Bible, the Church and the Reason*, before the delivery of the argument for the defense.

C. A. BRIGGS.

C.

Exception taken Dec. 22, 1892.

I beg leave to take exception to that part of the proceedings of the Presbytery of yesterday, recorded in the Stenographical Report, which permitted the Rev. Dr. Lampe, arguing in behalf of the prosecution, under the cloak of a rebuttal, to introduce new evidence, and new matter, and, in large measure, to reargue the Amended Charges and Specifications apart from and without regard to the Argument of the accused; in that (1) he introduced new evidence without the permission of Presbytery, and without notification to the accused, as follows: John Goodwin's *Divine Authority of the Scriptures;* Capel's *Remains;* Matthew Poole's *Commentary;* Baxter's *Reasons of the Christian Religion;* Chillingworth's *Works,* Vol. 1; Henry Hammond's *Paraphrases;* Lightfoot's *Difficulties of Scripture;* Timothy Dwight's *Sermons;* Jonathan Dickinson's *Sermons;* Samuel Davies' *Sermons;* Jonathan Edwards' *Works;* S. S. Smith's *Principles of Natural and Revealed Religion;* Sprague's *Annals;* McWhorter's *Sermons;* Witherspoon's *Works;* Ashbel Green's *Lectures on the Shorter Catechism;* Archibald Alexander's *Canon;* Gardiner Spring's *Bible not of Man;* Albert Barnes' *Commentaries;* Skinner's *Discussions in Theology;* Augustine's *Letters; Bibliotheca Sacra,* 1892; Liddon's *Divinity of our Lord.*

(2). In that he introduced new matter, as for example: an argument on verbal inspiration and dictation; an argument against an errant Bible; an argument against a statement of the Response; an argument against rationalistic critics; an argument from predictive prophecy; an argument against the theory of accommodation; an argument against the errancy of Jesus.

(3). In that he argued in more than two-thirds of his argument against the statements of the Inaugural Address, the Response to the original Charges, the Lectures on the Bible, the Church, and the Reason, and the other writings of the accused; and in not more than one-third of it can it be recognized as an effort in rebuttal of the argument of the accused; and in this part the argument can be considered as rebuttal only in so far as the argument for the defence included certain portions of *The Bible, the Church and the Reason;* and all of this with the exception of the two lines—"This is substantially the view of Dr. Briggs, as shown by the documents put in your hands by him" (p. 1241 Stenographical Report), and possibly of these also, was probably composed before the delivery of the Argument for the defence, for there is no other reference to that argument in the argument of Dr. Lampe yesterday.

C. A. BRIGGS.

D.

The Exception taken to the new matter included in Dr. Lampe's printed argument, but not delivered by him before the Presbytery, Dec. 22d, 1892.

Prof. BRIGGS—And now, Mr. Moderator, I wish to make a request of the Presbytery, namely, that they shall direct Dr. Lampe to specify what portions of the printed argument put in our hands have not been read on this floor. I make this request—not to exclude any part of his argument from consideration; if they wish to have it incorporated in the stenographic report, I for one shall make no objection—but it is necessary for me to know what I am to except to; and there are matters contained in this printed argument which were not read before us and which I want to except to and which I cannot except to unless they are recognized as before the court. Therefore, I request that Dr. Lampe shall specify what portions of his printed argument have not been presented to the court.

The MODERATOR—I think that is a proper request to make.

[After a few moments of discussion.]

The MODERATOR—Would not this relieve the diffi-culty: If Dr. Lampe be allowed to incorporate the printed form in the stenographer's notes, just as matter submitted by you has been incorporated?

Dr. BRIGGS—Yes, if the house will take the same action in this case as it took in my case. I think the house should take the action, however.

The MODERATOR—The question, then, is for the house to decide, namely, that Dr. Lampe has power to incor-porate in the stenographer's minutes the argument in printed form as presented, including the portions omitted in reading.

It was so ordered.

The Exception.

Inasmuch as the Presbytery gave Dr. Lampe "power to incorporate in the Stenographer's minutes the argu-ment in printed form as presented, including the por-tion omitted in reading," I beg leave to take exception to that part of the proceedings of the Presbytery which permitted Dr. Lampe, arguing in behalf of the prosecu-tion, under the cloak of a rebuttal to introduce new evidence as follows:

Alexander on *Isaiah;* Rawlinson in *Pulpit Commen-tary;* Ray, *Introduction,* in *Bible Commentary;* Manly's *Bible Doctrine of Inspiration; Hebraica,* October, 1888; Prof. John Kennedy, *A Popular Argument for the Unity of Isaiah,* 1891; Prof. John Forbes, *The Servant of the Lord in Israel,* xl–lxvi., 1890; Rector F. Watson, *The Law and the Prophets,* Hulsean Lecture for 1882; Prof. Stanley Leathes, *The Law in the Prophets,* 1891; Very Rev. R. Payne-Smith, *The Mosaic Authorship and Credi-bility of the Pentateuch,* 1869; James Sime, F.R.S.E.,

The Kingdom of all Israel, 1883; Prof. Robert Watts, *The Newer Criticism*, etc., 1882; Principal Rainy, *The Bible and Criticism*, 1878; Bishop A. C. Hervey, *The Books of Chronicles in Relation to the Pentateuch*, etc., 1892; Bishop C. J. Ellicott, *Christus Comprobator*, 1892; Rev. Henry Hayman, D.D., *Prophetic Testimony to the Pentateuch*, Bib. Sac., 1892; Pastor Tr. Roos, *Die Geschichtlichkeit des Pentateuchs*, 1883; Adolf Zahn, *Das Deuteronomium*, 1890; Eduard Böhl, *Zum Gesetz und zum Zeugniss*, 1883; Pastor G. Schumann, *Die Wellhausenische Hypothese*, 1892; R. S. Poole, *Date of the Pentateuch, Theory and Facts*, Cont. Review, 1887; Conder, *Ancient Men and Modern Critics*, Cont. Review, 1887; Edersheim, *Prophecy and History in Relation to the Messiah*, Warburton Lectures, 1880–84: Waller, *Is Genesis a Compilation?* Theological Monthly, 1891; Pastor Naumann, *Das Erste Buch der Bibel*, 1890; Prof. William H. Green, *Moses and the Pentateuch Vindicated;* Prof. E. Cone Bissell, *The Pentateuch;* Vos, *Mosaic Origin of the Pentateuch Codes*, 1886; Stebbins, *A Study of the Pentateuch*, 1881; S. C. Bartlett, *Sources of History in the Pentateuch*, Stone Lecture, 1882; Rabbi Wise, *Pronaos to Holy Writ*, 1891; Lias, *Wellhausen on the Pentateuch*, in the Theological Review, 1890.

C. A. BRIGGS.

E.

Exception taken December 28th, 1892.

I beg leave to take exception to that part of the proceedings of the Presbytery of Thursday last, recorded in the Stenographical Report, which permitted the Rev. Dr. Lampe, arguing in behalf of the prosecution, under the cloak of a rebuttal, to introduce new evidence, and new matter, and, in large measure, to reargue the

Amended Charges and Specifications apart from and without regard to the Argument of the accused ; in that (1). Dr. Lampe introduced new evidence without the permission of Presbytery, and without notification to the accused, as follows :

The Andover Review, vol. xiii. ; *Pepys' Diary;* F. Hall's *English Adjectives;* F. Hall's *Modern English.*

(2). In that Dr. Lampe introduced new matter, *e. g.,* an argument from the assumption that the ministry of the word will not continue in the next world, and an argument from the assumed instantaneous sanctification of believers at the second advent.

(3). In that Dr. Lampe argued for the most part against statements of the Inaugural Address, the Response to the Original Charges, the article " Redemption after Death," in the *Magazine of Christian Literature* ; many of which, such as those referring to race redemption, the moral character of Abraham, and the doctrine of election, were not included in the Amended Charges, and the argument of Dr. Lampe was not in any respect a rebuttal of the argument of the accused, of which argument the argument of Dr. Lampe on the sixth Charge seems entirely unconscious.

(4). In that Dr. Lampe argued on the seventh Charge of the Amended Charges, which the Presbytery directed the prosecution to remove from the list of Charges.

(5). In that Dr. Lampe argued that the accused was "under the influence of a philosophical principle of Naturalism," a matter not included in the Charges.

C. A. BRIGGS.

F.

The decision of the Moderator that the Prosecution had introduced new matter.

On December 22d there was considerable discussion whether the prosecution had introduced new matter into their argument on rebuttal. After Prof. Briggs had replied to this argument of the prosecution, the Moderator made the following decision :

" The Moderator is very clearly of the view, already embodied in his ruling, that the Prosecuting Committee had the right to open and to close, to be fully heard ; and that they should close, provided no new matter should be introduced. New matter having been introduced in the view of the Moderator, Dr. Briggs has now made reply. The Moderator's view is, and his decision is, that the case is now closed."

VII.

THE FINAL JUDGMENT OF THE PRESBYTERY.

A.—*The vote upon the Amended Charges and Specifications giving the final judgment of the Presbytery of New York, December 30, 1892.*

The votes are given upon each Specification and upon each item of the Charges. *N* indicates *not sustained*, and implies acquittal. *S* indicates *sustained*, and implies conviction.

A—MINISTERS.

MINISTERS.	I. Specif. 1	I. Specif. 2	I. Charge a.	I. Charge b.	II. Specif. 1	II. Specif. 2	II. Charge a.	II. Charge b.	III. Specif. 1	III. Charge a.	III. Charge b.	III. Charge c.	IV. Specif.	IV. Charge a.	IV. Charge b.	V. Specif.	V. Charge a.	V. Charge b.	VI. Specif.	VI. Charge
Alexander, Geo.	n	n	n	n	n	n	n	n	n	n	n	n	n	n	n	n	n	n	n	n
Alexander, S. D.	s	s	s	s	s	s	s	s	s	s	s	s	s	s	s	s	s	s	s	s
Arreghi, Antonio	n	n	n	n	n	n	n	n	n	n	n	n	n	n	n	n	n	n	s	s
Atterbury, A. P.	n	n	n	n	n	n	n	n	n	n	n	n	n	n	n	n	n	n	n	n
Atterbury, W. W.	n	n	n	n	n	n	n	n	n	n	n	n	n	n	n	n	n	n	n	n
Beebe, F. G	n	n	n	n	n	n	n	n	n	n	n	n	n	n	n	n	n	n	n	n
Bowden, Samuel	s	s	s	s	s	s	s	s	s	s	s	s	s	s	s	s	s	s	s	s
Bradner, T. S.	s	s	s	s	s	s	s	s	s	s	s	s	s	s	s	s	s	s	s	s
Brown, Francis	n	n	n	n	n	n	n	n	n	n	n	n	n	n	n	n	n	n	n	n
Buchanan, W. D.	s	s	s	s	s	s	s	s	s	s	s	s	s	s	s	s	s	s	s	s
Chambers, James	s	s	s	s	n	n	n	n	s	s	s	s	n	n	n	n	n	n	s	s
Clark, E. L.	n	n	n	n	n	n	n	n	n	n	n	n	n	n	n	n	n	n	n	n
Devins, J. B	s	s	s	s	n	n	n	n	s	s	s	s	s	s	s	s	s	s	n	n
Dodd, I. S.	n	n	n	n	n	n	n	n	n	n	n	n	n	n	n	n	n	n	n	n
Dodge, D. Stuart	n	n	n	n	n	n	n	n	n	n	n	n	n	n	n	n	n	n	n	n
Doench, C.	s	s	s	s	s	s	s	s	s	s	s	s	s	s	s	s	s	s	s	s
Durant, W.	n	n	n	n	n	n	n	n	n	n	n	n	n	n	n	n	n	n	n	n
Douglas, T.	s	s	s	s	s	s	s	s	s	s	s	s	s	s	s	s	s	s	s	s
Duffield, H.	s	s	s	s	s	s	s	s	s	s	s	s	s	s	s	s	s	s	s	s
Edwards, J. H.	n	n	n	n	n	n	n	n	n	n	n	n	n	n	n	n	n	n	n	n
Elliot, H. B.	s	s	s	s	s	s	s	s	s	s	s	s	s	s	s	s	s	s	s	s
Elsing, W. T.	n	n	n	n	n	n	n	n	n	n	n	n	n	n	n	n	n	n	n	n
Fagnani, C. P.	n	n	n	n	n	n	n	n	n	n	n	n	n	n	n	n	n	n	n	n
Field, H. M	n	n	n	n	n	n	n	n	n	n	n	n	n	n	n	n	n	n	n	n
Floyd, W. B.	s	s	s	s	s	s	s	s	s	s	s	s	s	s	s	s	s	s	s	s
Forbes, Jesse F.	n	n	n	n	n	n	n	n	n	n	n	n	n	n	n	n	n	n	n	n
Ford, H	n	n	n	n	n	n	n	n	n	n	n	n	n	n	n	n	n	n	n	n
Gillett, C. R.	n	n	n	n	n	n	n	n	n	n	n	n	n	n	n	n	n	n	n	n
Grandlienard, H. L.	n	n	n	n	n	n	n	n	n	n	n	n	n	n	n	n	n	n	n	n
Hall, James	s	s	s	s	s	s	s	s	s	s	s	s	s	s	s	s	s	s	s	s
Halsey, A. W.	n	n	n	n	n	n	n	n	n	n	n	n	n	n	n	n	n	n	n	n
Harshaw, W. R	n	n	n	n	n	n	n	n	n	n	n	n	n	n	n	n	n	n	n	n
Hastings, T. S	n	n	n	n	n	n	n	n	n	n	n	n	n	n	n	n	n	n	n	n
Hitchcock, E. W.	n	n	n	n	n	n	n	n	n	n	n	n	n	n	n	n	n	n	n	n
Hoadley, J. H.	n	n	n	n	n	n	n	n	n	n	n	n	n	n	n	n	n	n	n	n
Hunter, J.	n	n	n	n	n	n	n	n	n	n	n	n	n	n	n	n	n	n	n	n
Jackson, S M.	n	n	n	n	n	n	n	n	n	n	n	n	n	n	n	n	n	n	n	n
Jewett, A. D. L.	s	s	s	s	s	s	s	s	s	s	s	s	s	s	s	s	s	s	s	s
Kerr, Jos. R	n	n	n	n	n	n	n	n	n	n	n	n	n	n	n	n	n	n	n	n
King, Albert B.									s	s	s	s	s	s	s	s	s	s	s	s
King, A. D	s	s	s	s	s	s	s	s	s	s	s	s							s	s
Leonhard, Theo.	n	n	n	n	n	n	n	n	n	n	n	n	n	n	n	n	n	n	n	n

(155)

A—MINISTERS.

MINISTERS.	I Specif. 1	I Specif. 2	I Charge a.	I Charge b.	II Specif. 1	II Specif. 2	II Charge a.	II Charge b.	III Specif. 1	III Charge a.	III Charge b.	III Charge c.	IV Specif.	IV Charge a.	IV Charge b.	V Specif.	V Charge a.	V Charge b.	VI Specif.	VI Charge.
Littlefield, M. S.	n	n	n	n	n	n	n	n	n	n	n	n	n	n	n	n	n	n	n	n
Lowrie, J. C.	s	s	s	s	s	s	s	s	s	s	s	s	s	s	s	s	s	s	s	s
Lorenz, D. E.	n	n	n	n	n	n	n	n	n	n	n	n	n	n	n	n	n	n	n	n
Martin, W. M.	n	n	n	n	n	n	n	n	n	n	n	n	n	n	n	n	n	n	n	n
Mallery, C. P.	s	s	s	s	s	s	s	s	s	s	s	s	s	s	s	s	s	s	s	s
Marling, F. H.	n	n	n	n	n	n	n	n	n	n	n	n	n	n	n	n	n	n	n	n
McEwen, H. T.	n	n	n	n	n	n	n	n	n	n	n	n	n	n	n	n	n	n	n	n
McIlvaine, J. H.	n	n	n	n	n	n	n	n	n	n	n	n	n	n	n	n	n	n	n	n
McKinney, Alex	n	n	n	n	n	n	n	n	n	n	n	n	n	n	n	n	n	n	n	n
McLean, Alex	s	s	s	s	s	s	s	s	s	s	s	s	s	s	s	s	s	s	s	s
McMillan, D. J.	n	n	n	n	n	n	n	n	n	n	n	n	n	n	n	n	n	n	n	n
Miller, H. G	s	s	s	s	s	s	s	s	s	s	s	s	s	s	s	s	s	s	s	s
Mingins, G. J	n	n	n	n	n	n	n	n	n	n	n	n	n	n	n	n	n	n	n	n
Moore, W. L.	s	s	s	s	s	s	s	s	s	s	s	s	s	s	s	s	s	s	s	s
Nightingale. J. C.	s	s	s	s	s	s	s	s	s	s	s	s	s	s	s	s	s	s	s	s
Nixon, Geo.	s	s	s	s	s	s	s	s	s	s	s	s	s	s	s	s	s	s	s	s
Northrup, I. H.	s	s	s	s	s	s	s	s	s	s	s	s	s	s	s	s	s	s	s	s
Overton, D. H.	n	n	n	n	n	n	n	n	n	n	n	n	n	n	n	n	n	n	n	n
Parsons, L. H.	s	s	s	s	s	s	s	s	s	s	s	s	s	s	s	s	s	s	s	s
Patterson, J. G.	s	s	s	s	s	s	s	s	s	s	s	s	s	s	s	s	s	s	s	s
Payson, E. P.	s	s	s	s	s	s	s	s	s	s	s	s	s	s	s	s	s	s	s	s
Payson, G. S.	n	n	n	n	n	n	n	n	n	n	n	n	n	n	n	n	n	n	n	n
Pisek, V.	n	n	n	n	n	n	n	n	n	n	n	n	n	n	n	n	n	n	n	n
Pritchard, Hugh	s	s	s	s	s	s	s	s	s	s	s	s	s	s	s	s	s	s	n	s
Ramsay, J. S.	n	n	n	n	n	n	n	n	s	s	n	s	s	n	n	n	n	n	n	s
Redmon, D.	n	n	n	n	n	n	n	n	n	n	n	n	n	n	n	n	n	n	n	n
Robinson, C. S	s	s	s	s	s	s	s	s	s	s	s	s				s			s	s
Rossiter, S. B.	n	n	n	n	n	n	n	n	n	n	n	n	n	n	n	n	n	n	n	n
Ruliffson, A. G.	s	s	s	s	s	s	s	s	s	s	s	s	s	s	n	n	n	n	n	s
Rice, W. A.	n	n	n	n	n	n	n	n	n	n	n	n	n	n	n	n	n	n	n	n
Sanderson, Jos.	s	s	s	s	s	s	s	s	s	s	s	s	s	s	s	s	s	s	n	s
Saxton, J. A.	n	n	n	n	n	n	n	n	n	n	n	n	n	n	n	n	n	n	n	n
Schaff, P.	n	n	n	n	n	n	n	n	n	n	n	n	n	n	n	n	n	n	n	n
Shaw, J. B.	n	n	n	n	n	n	n	n	n	n	n	n	n	n	n	n	n	n	n	n
Shearer, Geo. L.	s	s	s	s	s	s	s	s	s	s	s	s	s	s	s	s	s	s	s	s
Shiland, A.	s	s	s	s	s	s	s	s	s	s	s	s	s	s	s	s	s	s	s	s
Smith, W. M	n	n	n	n	n	n	n	n	n	n	n	n	n	n	n	n	n	n	n	n
Stitt, W. C.	s	s	s	s	s	s	s	s	s	s	s	s	s	s	s	n	n	n	s	s
Stoddard, C. A.	n	s	s	s	s	s	s	s	s	s	s	s	n	n	n	n	n	n	s	s
Sutton, J. F.	s	s	s	s	s	s	s	s	s	s	s	s	s	s	s	s	s	s	s	s
Sproull, A. W.	s	s	s	s	s	s	s	s	s	s	s	s	s	s	s	s	s	s	s	s
Spining, G. L.	n	n	n	n	n	n	n	n	n	n	n	n	n	n	n	n	n	n	n	n
Thompson, C. L.	n	n	n	n	n	n	n	n	n	n	n	n	n	n	n	n	n	n	n	n
Thompson, J. J.	s	s	s	s	s	s	s	s	s	s	s	s	s	s	s				n	s
Tyndall, H. M.	s	s	s	s	s	s	s	s	s	s	s	s	s	s	s	s	s	s	n	s
Van Dyke, H.	n	n	n	n	n	n	n	n	n	n	n	n	n	n	n	n	n	n	n	n
Vincent, M. R.	n	n	n	n	n	n	n	n	n	n	n	n	n	n	n	n	n	n	n	n
Voegelin, F. E.	s	s	s	s	s	s	s	s	s	s	s	s	s	s	s	s	s	s	s	s
Wall, T. G.	s	s	s	s	s	s	s	s	s	s	s	s	s	s	s	s	s	s	s	s
Waite, A. L. R.	s	s	s	s	s	s	s	s	s	s	s	s	s	s	s				s	s
Watson, W. S.	n	n	n	n	n	n	n	n	s	s	n	s	s	s	s	s	s	s	s	s
Webster, G. S.	n	n	n	n	n	n	n	n	n	n	n	n	n	n	n	n	n	n	n	n
White, E. N.	n	n	n	n	n	n	n	n	n	n	n	n	n	n	n	n	n	n	n	n
Willard, L.	s	s	s	s																
Wylie D. G.	s	s	s	s	s	s	s	s	s	s	s	s	n	n	n	n	n	n	s	s
No. of votes "not sustained"	55	54	54	54	56	56	56	56	52	52	54	52	55	55	55	57	57	57	55	55
No. of votes "sustained."	41	42	42	42	39	39	39	39	44	44	42	44	39	39	39	35	35	35	41	41

B—ELDERS.

Churches	Elders	I Sp.1	I Sp.2	I Ch.a	I Ch.b	II Sp.1	II Sp.2	II Ch.a	II Ch.b	III Sp.1	III Ch.a	III Ch.b	III Ch.c	IV Sp.	IV Ch.a	IV Ch.b	V Sp.	V Ch.a	V Ch.b	VI Sp.	VI Ch.
ethany	Tompkins, Jas	s	s	s	s	s	s	s	s	s	s	s	s	s	s	s	s	s	s	s	s
rick	Ledoux, A. R.	n	n	n	n	n	n	n	n	n	n	n	n	n	n	n	n	n	n	n	n
alvary	Ketchum, A. P.	s	s	s	s	n	n	n	n	s	s	s	s	n	n	n	n	n	n	s	s
entral	Mickens, Wm	n	n	n	n	n	n	n	n	n	n	n	n	n	n	n	n	n	n	n	n
hrist.	Robinson, Andrew	s	s	s	s	s	s	s	s	s	s	s	s	s	s	s	s	s	s	s	s
. Harlem	McDowell, Jas	s	s	s	s	s	s	s	s	s	s	s	s	s	s	s	s	s	s	s	s
th Ave	Rowland, H. E.	s	s	s	s	s	s	s	s	s	s	s	s	s	s	s	s	s	s	s	s
irst	McJimpsey, E.	s	s	s	s	s	s	s	s	s	s	s	s	s	s	s	s	s	s	s	s
ourth	McWilliam, Jno	s	s	s	s	s	s	s	s	s	s	s	s	s	s	s					
h Ave	Sterry, Geo. E.	s	s	s	s	s	s	s	s	s	s	s	s	s	s	s	s	s	s	s	s
th St.	Reeve, Samuel	n	n	n	n	n	n	n	n	n	n	n	n	n	n	n	n	n	n	n	n
arlem	Willard, S H	s	s	s	s	s	s	s	s	s	s	s	s	s	s	s	s	s	s	s	s
nox	Moorhead, Jos	s	s	s	s	s	s	s	s	s	s	s	s	s	s	s	s	s	s	s	s
adison Sq	Woodbury, C. H.	n	n	n	n	n	n	n	n	n	n	n	n	n	n	n	n	n	n	n	n
orrisania, 1st.	Johnson, Robert	n	n	n	n	n	n	n	n	n	n	n	n	n	n	n	n	n	n		
ew York	Anderson, Thomas	s	s	s	s	s	s	s	s	s	s	s	s	s	s	s	s	s	s	s	s
orth	King, G. C.	n	n	n	n	n	n	n	n	n	n	n	n	n	n	n	n	n	n	n	n
ark	Hawley, H. Q.	n	n	n	n	n	n	n	n	n	n	n	n	n	n	n	n	n	n	n	n
hillips	Ware, Jas. E.	n	n	n	n	n	n	n	n	n	n	n	n	n	n	n	n	n	n	n	n
uritans	Lay, Geo. C.	n	n	n	n	n	n	n	n	n	n	n	n	n	n	n	n	n	n	n	n
iverdale	Dodge, C. H.	n	n	n	n	n	n	n	n	n	n	n	n	n	n	n	n	n	n	n	n
utgers	Onderdonk, W. H.	s	s	s	s	s	s	s	s	s	s	s	s	s	s	s	s	s	s	s	s
cotch	Houston, Robert	s	s	s	s	s	s	s	s	s	s	s	s	s	s	s	s	s	s	s	s
eventh	Anderson, Jas	s	s	s	s	s	s	s	s	s	s	s	s	s	s	s	s	s	s	s	s
th St	Worrall, Wm. R.	s	s	s	s	s	s	s	s	s	s	s	s	s	s	s	s	s	s	s	s
remont	Garey, C. E.	s	s	s	s	s	s	s	s	s	s	s	s	n	n	n				s	s
niversity Pl	Bond, Thos	n	n	n	n	n	n	n	n	n	n	n	n	n	n	n	n	n	n	n	n
nion Tabern	Gentle, Robert	n	n	n	n	n	n	n	n	n	n	n	n	n	n	n	n	n	n	n	n
ash. Heights	Wheelock, W. A.	n	n	n	n	n	n	n	n	n	n	n	n	n	n	n	n	n	n	n	n
est	Jaffray, Robert	n	n	n	n	n	n	n	n	n	n	n	n	n	n	n	n	n	n	n	n
est End	Leggett, C. P.	n	n	n	n	n	n	n	n	n	n	n	n	n	n	n	n	n	n	n	n
estminster	Drummond, R.	s	s	s	s	s	s	s	s	s	s	s	s	s	s	s	s	s	s	s	s
	No. of votes "not sustained"	15	15	15	15	16	16	16	16	15	15	15	15	17	17	17	16	16	16	14	14
	No. of votes "sustained"	17	17	17	17	16	16	16	16	17	17	17	17	15	15	15	14	14	14	16	16

Total.	I Sp.1	I Sp.2	I Ch.a	I Ch.	II Sp.1	II Sp.2	II Ch.a	II Ch.b	III Sp.1	III Ch.a	III Ch.b	III Ch.c	IV Sp.	IV Ch.a	IV Ch.b	V Sp.	V Ch.a	V Ch.b	VI Sp.	VI Ch.
"Not sustained"	70	69	69	69	72	72	72	72	67	67	69	67	72	72	72	73	73	73	69	69
"Sustained"	58	59	59	59	55	55	55	55	61	61	59	61	54	54	54	49	49	49	57	57
stain	12	10	10	10	17	17	17	17	6	6	10	6	18	18	18	24	24	24	12	12

gs had been
ery, he then
rmulate the

B. *The Judgment of the Presbytery, Jan. 9th,* 1893.

The Committee appointed to bring in the result of the vote and the judgment of the judicatory begs leave to report as follows :

The case of the Presbyterian Church in the United States of America against the Rev. Chas. A. Briggs, D.D., having been dismissed by the Presbytery of New York on November 4th, 1891, was remanded by the General Assembly of 1892 to the same Presbytery with instructions that " it be brought to issue and tried on the merits thereof as speedily as possible."

In obedience to this mandate the Presbytery of New York has tried the case. It has listened to the evidence and argument of the Committee of Prosecution acting in fidelity to the duty committed to them. It has heard the defence and evidence of the Rev. Charles A. Briggs, D.D., presented in accordance with the rights secured to every minister of the Church.

The Presbytery has kept in mind these established principles of our polity " that no man can rightly be convicted of heresy by inference or implication "; that in the interpretation of " ambiguous expressions " " candor requires that a court should favor the accused by putting upon his words the more favorable rather than the less favorable construction "; and that " there are truths and forms with respect to which men of good character may differ."

Giving due consideration to the defendant's explanations of the language used in his Inaugural Address, accepting his frank and full disclaimer of the interpretation which has been put upon some of its phrases and illustrations, crediting his affirmations of loyalty to the standards of the Church and to the Holy Scriptures as the only infallible rule of faith and practice, the Presbytery does not find that he has transgressed the limits of liberty allowed under our Constitution to scholarship and opinion.

Therefore, without expressing approval of the critical or theological views embodied in the Inaugural Address, or the manner in which they have been expressed and illustrated, the Presbytery pronounces the Rev. Charles A. Briggs, D.D., fully acquitted of the offences alleged against him—the several charges and specifications accepted for probation having been "not-sustained" by the following vote:

		SUSTAINED.			NOT SUSTAINED.		
		MINISTERS.	ELDERS.	TOTAL.	MINISTERS.	ELDERS.	TOTAL.
I.	1 Specification	41	17	58	55	15	70
	2 "	42	17	59	54	15	69
	Charge { a.	42	17	59	54	15	69
	{ b.	42	17	59	54	15	69
II.	1 Specification	39	16	55	56	16	72
	2 "	39	16	55	56	16	72
	Charge { a.	39	16	55	56	16	72
	{ b.	39	16	55	56	16	72
III.	Specification	44	17	61	52	15	67
	Charge { a.	44	17	61	52	15	67
	{ b.	42	17	59	54	15	69
	{ c.	44	17	61	52	15	67
IV.	Specification..	39	15	54	55	17	72
	Charge { a.	39	15	54	55	17	72
	{ b.	39	15	54	55	17	72
V.	Specification	35	14	49	57	16	73
	Charge { a.	35	14	49	57	16	73
	{ b.	35	14	49	57	16	73
VI.	Specification	41	16	57	55	14	69
	Charge	41	16	57	55	14	69

The above is the correct vote.

Accordingly, the Presbytery, making full recognition of the ability, sincerity and patience with which the Committee of Prosecution have performed the onerous duty assigned to them, does now, to the extent of its constitutional power, relieve said Committee from further responsibility in connection with this case.

In so doing the Presbytery is not undertaking to decide how far that Committee is subject to the authority of the body appointing it, but intends by this action to express an earnest conviction that the grave issues involved in this case will be more wisely and justly determined by calm investigation and fraternal discussion than by judicial arraignment and process.

In view of the present disquietude in the Presbyterian Church, and of the obligation resting upon all Christians to have tender concern for the consciences of their brethren, the Presbytery earnestly counsels its members to avoid, on the one hand, hasty or over-confident statement of private opinion on points concerning which profound and reverent students of God's Word are not yet agreed, and, on the other, suspicions and charges of false teaching which are not clearly capable of proof.

Moreover, the Presbytery advises and exhorts all subject to its authority to regard the many and great things in which we agree rather than the few and minor things in which we differ, and turning from the paths of controversy, to devote their energies to the great and urgent work of the Church which is the proclamation of the Gospel and the edifying of the Body of Christ.

(Signed),

GEORGE ALEXANDER,
HENRY VAN DYKE,
ROBERT JAFFRAY.

A Resolution to lay the second section on the table was lost by a vote of 47 to 58; after which the Report was adopted in its several parts. Whereupon the Report was adopted as a whole by a majority vote, and the Moderator declared that this be the judgment of the Court, and that it be entered accordingly.

The Higher Criticism of the Hexateuch.

By CHARLES AUGUSTUS BRIGGS, D.D., Edward Robinson Professor of Biblical Theology in the Union Theological Seminary, New York.   Crown octavo, $1.75.

The most prominent exponent of the Higher Criticism of the Hebrew Scriptures in America is Professor Briggs.   If he is not at the same time the most learned and fully equipped scholar among us in this field, it would not be easy to name his peer.   For many years his contributions to the literature of the subject in the great theological reviews have been widely read and have been the object of much criticism from the adherents of the opposite school.   Owing to the prominence and the great importance of the trial to which he has been subjected because of his views on Old Testament Criticism, his interpretation of the principles that he champions is of the highest consequence.

Many years ago he began the preparation of a book on the Higher Criticism of the Hexateuch, but deeming the times not yet ripe for it, it was laid aside for other work.   The events of the past few months render it necessary for the author to define his position in regard to the Hexateuch, and for this reason he publishes this volume, which presents the result of his studies and includes a large amount of fresh evidence, which now appears for the first time.

The results of his researches correspond, in the main, with the opinions which have been formed independently by leading Biblical scholars in all parts of the world.   But it is now time that these questions should no longer be confined to theological schools and professional circles.   It is with the aim of contributing to the readjustment of opinions and to a better understanding and higher appreciation of the documents of the Bible that the book has been written, which is designed for the general public rather than for Hebrew students, and, for the most part, technical material has been put in the Appendix, which constitutes a considerable part of the volume.

The Bible, the Church, and the Reason.

The Three Great Fountains of Divine Authority. By CHARLES A. BRIGGS, D.D., Edward Robinson Professor of Biblical Theology in Union Theological Seminary, New York. Crown octavo, $1.75.

" It consists of lectures delivered at different times since the recent assault upon him. In these lectures he does not indicate the least inclination to beat a retreat, cry for quarter, or even secure a truce. And yet, with some few exceptions, he does not exhibit personal feeling, nor defend himself personally from the charges made against him. He simply elaborates and substantiates the positions in his inaugural which have subjected him to public criticism and to a possible trial for heresy."—*The Christian Union.*

" The problems which are discussed with masterly power in this volume are not those of Presbyterianism, or of Protestantism, but of Christianity, and, indeed, of all Biblical religion. To any man for whom the question of God and revelation has an endlessly fascinating interest, the book will prove suggestive and stimulating. We cannot see why even the Israelite and the Roman Catholic should not desire to taste—despite the traditions of synagogue and Mother Church—this latest forbidden fruit of the tree of knowledge."—*The Literary World.*

" But on a calm review of this book, while making due allowance for some of the characterizations of his opponents, and without entering into the merits of the subject involved, one must reach the candid conclusion that Professor Briggs is deeply reverent and devout in his attitude towards the Word of God ; that he is conscientiously and earnestly aiming at its exaltation and its stronger hold upon the minds and hearts of men. He says : 'Criticism makes the Bible more real, more historic, more pregnant with holy meaning than ever before. . . . . Think not the critics are destroying the Bible which they study with so much enthusiasm and love. They have enthroned it in a higher position than it has ever held before in the estimation of the world.' Surely, an impartial judgment will not fail to give full credit for purity of motive and loftiness of purpose to a man who writes like this."—*The Evangelist.*

" It deals, as the author observes, with 'matters which lie at the root of our common Christianity,' and largely, at any rate, 'with questions of truth and fact,' to be determined, not by hasty and superficial writers in periodicals, but 'by patient, diligent, painstaking, exhaustive investigation of truth and fact.' (Preface p. ix.) It appeals, therefore, to men of all shades of churchmanship, provided that they recognize the duty of continually absorbing fresh elements of truth, which both may and must more or less modify the conceptions already adopted by the common consent of past ages. But, if I may say so, it appeals most of all to those who attach the highest value to the principles of the Reformation, and who, therefore, recognize a Bible within the Bible, of which the experience of the Christian life in the community and in the individual is the true test."—*Professor T. K. Cheyne, D.D., in the London Academy.*

Biblical Study.

Its Principles, Methods, and History, together with a Catalogue of Books of Reference. By CHARLES A. BRIGGS, D.D., Edward Robinson Professor of Biblical Theology in the Union Theological Seminary, New York. Fourth Edition. One volume, crown 8vo, $2.50.

"A choice book, for which we wish wide circulation and deep influence in its own land and also recognition among us. The author maintains his position with so much spirit and in such beautiful language that his book makes delightful reading, and it is particularly instructive for Germans on account of the very characteristic extracts from the writings of English theologians of the seventeenth and eighteenth centuries. Moreover, he is unusually familiar with German literature of recent date as well as with that of the earlier period."—*Zarncke's Literaturisches Centralblatt für Deutschland.*

"Here is a theological writer, thoroughly scientific in his methods, and yet not ashamed to call himself evangelical. One great merit of this handbook is the light which it throws on the genesis of modern criticism and exegesis. Those who use it will escape the crudities of many English advocates of half-understood theories. Not the least of its merits is the well-selected catalogue of books of reference—English, French, and German. We are sure that no student will regret sending for the book."—*The Academy*, London.

"Dr. Briggs begins with a chapter upon the advantages of Biblical study, and the subjects of the following chapters are: Exegetical Theology, the Languages of the Bible, the Bible and Criticism, the Canon and Text of the Bible, Higher Criticism, Literary Study of the Bible, Hebrew Poetry, Interpretation of Scripture, Biblical Theology, and the Scriptures as a Means of Grace. It will be seen that the subjects occupy a wide range, and, ably treated as they are, the volume becomes one of real value and utility. Appended to the work is a valuable catalogue of books of reference in biblical studies, and three indexes—of Scriptures, of topics, and of books and authors. The publishers have done honor to the work, and it deserved it."—*The Churchman.*

"The minister who thoroughly masters this volume will find himself mentally invigorated, as well as broadened in his scope of thought; will almost certainly be able to better satisfy himself in his understanding of what the truth is which from the Bible he ought to preach to men; and so will speak from his pulpit with new force, and find his words mightier, through God, to the pulling down of strongholds."—*Boston Congregationalist.*

"After all that we have heard of the higher criticism, it is refreshing to find so scholarly and trenchant defences of the old paths. . . . . His historical account of the movement and developement among the English-speaking scholars is very valuable. This, and the chapter on the 'Literary Study of the Bible,' are among the best in this excellent book."—*New York Christian Advocate* (Methodist).

"We are constrained to rank this book as one of the signs of the times in the American church. It marks the rising tide of Biblical scholarship, Christian liberty of thought and evangelical interpretation of the Scriptures."—*Christian Union.*

"There are many grounds on which the work may be earnestly commended. Large reading in German and English, quick apprehension of the salient points of opposing theories, an unflagging earnestness of purpose, and very positive belief in his positions conspire to make the work instructive and attractive. But above all these excellences there shines out the author's deep reverence for the whole Bible."—*The Examiner* (Baptist, N. Y.)

Messianic Prophecy.

The Prediction of the fulfilment of Redemption through the Messiah. A critical study of the Messianic passages of the Old Testament in the order of their development. By CHARLES A. BRIGGS, D.D., Edward Robinson Professor of Biblical Theology in the Union Theological Seminary, New York. One volume, crown octavo, $2.50.

"Messianic Prophecy is a subject of no common interest, and this book is no ordinary book. It is, on the contrary, a work of the very first order, the ripe product of years of study upon the highest themes. It is exegesis in master-hand, about its noblest business. . . . . It has been worth while to commend this book at some-length to the attention of Bible students, because both the subject and the treatment entitle it to rank among the very foremost works of the generation in the department of Exegetical Theology. Union Seminary is to be congratulated that it is one of her Professors who, in a noble line of succession has produced it. The American Church is to be congratulated that the author is an American, and Presbyterians that he is a Presbyterian. A Church that can yield such books has large possibilities."—*New York Evangelist.*

"It is second in importance to no theological work which has appeared in this country during the present century."—*The Critic.*

"His arduous labor has been well expended, for he has finally produced a book which will give great pleasure to Christians of all denominations. . . . . The profound learning displayed in the book commends it to the purchase of all clergymen who wish for the most critical and exact exposition of a difficult theme ; while its earnestness and eloquence will win for it a place in the library of every devout layman."—*N. Y. Journal of Commerce.*

"It is rich with the fruits of years of zealous and unwearied study, and of an ample learning. In it we have the first English work on Messianic Prophecy which stands on the level of modern Biblical studies, It is one of the most important and valuable contributions of American scholarships to those studies. It is always more than instructive : it is spiritually helpful. We commend the work not only to ministers, but to intelligent laymen."—*The Independent.*

"On the pervading and multiform character of this promise, see a recent, as well as valuable authority, in the volume of Dr. Briggs, of the New York Theological Seminary, on 'Messianic Prophecy.'"—W. E. GLADSTONE.

"Prof. Briggs' Messianic Prophecy is a most excellent book, in which I greatly rejoice."—Prof. FRANZ DELITZSCH.

"All scholars will join in recognizing its singular usefulness as a text-book. It has been much wanted."—Rev. CANON CHEYNE.

"It is a book that will be consulted and prized by the learned, and that will add to the author's deservedly high reputation for scholarship. Evidences of the ability, learning and patient research of the author are apparent from the beginning to the end of the volume, while the style is remarkably fine."—*Phila. Presbyterian.*

"His new book on Messianic Phrophecy is a worthy companion to his indispensable text-book on Biblical study . . . . What is most of all required to insure the future of Old Testament studies in this country is that those who teach should satisfy their students of their historic connection with the religion and theology of the past. Prof. Briggs has the consciousness of such a connection in a very full degree, and yet he combines this with a frank and unreserved adhesion to the principles of modern criticisms. . . . . He has produced the first English text-book on the subject of Messianic Prophecy which a modern teacher can use."—*The London Academy.*

Whither?

A Theological Question for the Times   By CHARLES AUGUSTUS
BRIGGS, D.D., Edward Robinson Professor of Biblical Theology
in the Union Theological Seminary, New York.   Third Edition.
One volume, crown 8vo, $1.75.

"He shows that genuine Christianity has nothing to lose, but much to gain, by un-
fettered thought and by the ripest modern scholarship ; that the doctrines which progressive theology threatens are no essential part of the historic faith, but rather out-
worn garments, woven with warp and woof of tradition and speculation ; that being
hung upon the noble form of Christianity, have obscured its real proportions, and
that 'the higher criticism ' of which timid and unscholarly souls are so much afraid,
is really making the Bible more manifestly the book of God, by relieving it from the
false interpretations of men."—*The Press*, Philadelphia.

"The book is a strong one. It is packed with weighty matter. Its reach is larger
than any of the author's other works, though its compass is smaller. It contains only
300 pages, yet it is a critical treatise on Westminster and modern theology, and also
on church life and Christian unity. It is written in nervous, virile English that holds
attention. It has unusual grasp and force. The title and the chapter headings suggest compression : 'Whither?' 'Drifting,' 'Orthodoxy,' 'Changes,' 'Shifting,'
'Excesses,' 'Failures,' 'Departures,' 'Perplexities,' 'Barriers,' 'Thither.' There
is a whole history in some of these words, and a whole sermon in others."—*The
Critic*, New York.

"At the same time it is irenic both in tone and tendency. It is noble from
beginning to end, though the author may possibly place unnecessary emphasis on
the organic unity of the different denominations of Christendom as the condition
precedent for a true catholic unity. There is not a touch or smell of rationalism or
rationalistic speculation in the book, and freely as the author deals with his opponents, it is an honest freedom, which will promote good feeling even amid debate."—
The Independent.

American Presbyterianism :

Its Origin and Early History, together with an Appendix of Letters and Documents, many of which have recently been discovered.
By CHARLES A. BRIGGS, D.D., Edward Robinson Professor of
Biblical Theology in the Union Theological Seminary, New York.
1 volume, crown 8vo, with Maps. $3.00.

"The Presbyterian Church owes a debt of gratitude to the enthusiasm and antiquar-
ian research of Professor Briggs. He seems to have seized the foremost place among
them, and his vigorous, skilful, and comprehensive researches put all Protestant
Christians, and especially Congregationalists, under obligation to him."—*Boston
Congregationalist.*

"This is an admirable and exhaustive work, full of vigorous thinking, clear and
careful statement, incisive and judicious criticism, minute yet comprehensive research.
It is such a book as only a man with a gift for historical inquiry and an enthusiasm
for the history and principles of his Church could have produced. It represents an
amazing amount of labor. Dr. Briggs seems to have searched every available source,
British and American, for printed or written documents bearing on his subjects, and
he has met with wonderful success. He has made many important discoveries, illustrative of the Puritan men and period, useful to himself, but certain also to be helpful
to all future inquiries in this field."—*British Quarterly Review.*

CHARLES SCRIBNER'S SONS, Publishers,
743 and 745 Broadway, New York.

Lightning Source UK Ltd.
Milton Keynes UK
UKHW010828211218
334381UK00013B/1059/P